At Issue

D0947480

How Valuable Is a College Degree?

Other Books in the At Issue Series:

Contents

Introduction

Debate about the value of a college degree has increased recently, in large part due to the rising cost of college attendance. The question of value is one that is partially assessed by weighing the cost of college attendance against the lifetime wage premium that results from having a college degree. A simplistic initial calculation might then look like this:

1. Assess the likely increase in earnings over a lifetime from having a college degree;

2. Subtract the cost of attending college for four years at the school in question, including income lost by not working those four years, and including any interest that will need to be paid back for student loans;

3. If the result is positive, the college degree wins out in value. If the result is negative, however, college is not a good value.

Nonetheless, there are other factors influencing the question of value. Going to college may have benefits that cannot be computed in terms of income, or even any monetary return: it may be the case that the experience of college itself has value to individuals whether or not it results in greater economic rewards. Of course, it may also be the case that college attendance has a negative noneconomic value if it squelches creativity or kills individuality. Thus, any assessment of the value of a college degree must also take stock of non-monetary rewards and burdens. Regardless, if the price of college attendance gets high enough to result in severe negative economic results, it may not matter how much nonmonetary value it has to individuals.

There is no doubt that the cost of college attendance has risen in recent decades. According to a 2015 report by the US

Department of Education's National Center for Education Statistics, the cost of college has more than doubled over the past thirty years. In 2012–13, the average total tuition, fees, and room and board rates charged for full-time undergraduates (across all institutions) equaled $20,234. Calculated in constant 2012–13 dollars, the average total tuition, fees, and room and board rates charged for full-time undergraduates thirty years prior, in 1982–83, totaled $9,138. The average yearly cost is much higher at private nonprofit and for-profit institutions than it is at public institutions, although the percentage increase is similar. For public institutions, the average yearly cost went from $6,941 in 1982–83 to $15,022 in 2012–13. At private nonprofit and for-profit institutions, the average yearly cost went from $16,311 in 1982–83 to $34,483 in 2012–13. In all instances the average yearly cost more than doubled during that thirty-year period.

Yet, the total cost of college tuition, fees, and room and board is not the amount each student pays. This amount does not include books, supplies, transportation, and living expenses, so these expenses need to be included in any assessment of the total costs of attending college. On the flip side, this amount may be reduced by scholarships or grants, which the student does not have to pay back. In addition, the student may take out loans to help pay for these costs so that the actual out-of-pocket yearly amount to attend college becomes lower. Nonetheless, the loans—unlike grants and scholarships—do need to be repaid after leaving college (whether one graduates or not), so they must be considered in the total cost. The US Department of Education's National Center for Education Statistics looked at how much students paid for the total cost of annual college attendance (including these other living costs beyond tuition, fees, and room and board) in 2011–12 after subtracting grants and scholarships. The net amount paid after grants and scholarships was quite a bit less than the total cost: $27,900 instead of $43,500 for private nonprofit schools; $25,200 instead of $29,300 at for-profit schools; $18,000 instead of $23,200 at public four-year schools; and $11,700 instead of $15,000 at public two-year schools. The amounts paid out-of-pocket were lower still after taking into account student loans.

Despite the increase in the cost of obtaining a college degree, the vast majority of Americans continue to believe that a college education is very important. Gallup began polling the American public on this issue in 1978. In that year, only 36 percent said that a college education was very important, with 46 percent saying it was fairly important and 16 percent saying it was not too important. In 2013—thirty-five years later—a whopping 70 percent of Americans said that obtaining a college education was very important, 23 percent said that it was fairly important, and only 6 percent said that it was not too important.

It is in this climate, with the cost of college attendance higher than ever and with public opinion stronger than ever on the value of a college education, that the authors of the viewpoints in this volume debate the value of a college degree. The poor job market for everyone, including college graduates, in the years since the Great Recession has added another dimension to the issue. As the viewpoints in *At Issue: How Valuable Is a College Degree?* illustrate, there is fierce debate about just how valuable a college degree is at this point in time.

1

The Rising Cost of *Not* Going to College

Pew Research Center

Pew Research Center is a nonpartisan fact tank that informs the public about the issues, attitudes, and trends shaping America and the world.

College graduates express greater job satisfaction and career success than those who did not graduate from college. College graduates overwhelming say that their education has been useful in preparing them for a job and most believe that their college degree has paid off.

For today's young workers, the surest path to a good job and satisfying career runs through college. A recent survey by the Pew Research Center finds that college graduates outpace those with less education on virtually every measure of job satisfaction and career success.

While most workers say their education has been at least somewhat helpful on the job, fully 47% of college graduates[1] ages 25 to 32 report that their schooling has been "very useful" in getting them ready for a job or career.

In contrast, only about a third (34%) of young adults with a high school education or less say their education has been as helpful to them, the survey found.

1. Unless otherwise noted in this report, "college graduate" refers to those who have a bachelor's degree or more education.

When it comes to their current jobs, about half (53%) of all employed college graduates in their mid-20s and early 30s say they are "very satisfied" at work. In contrast, only 37% of comparably aged Millennials with a high school diploma or less are as satisfied with their job, according to the Pew Research survey.

Employed college graduates ages 25 to 32 also are more likely than those with only a high school diploma or less to say they are in a career or career-track job (86% vs. 57%) and less likely to say their current job is just something "to get [them] by" (14% vs. 42%).

When they look ahead, about six-in-ten (63%) Millennial college graduates in their late 20s and early 30s are confident that they have enough training and education to get ahead in their current job or career. In contrast, about four-in-ten (41%) of comparably aged high school graduates feel they have enough education to advance on the job.

Even though the current Millennials ages 25 to 32 are better educated than the generations of young adults who preceded them,[2] the survey found only one significant generational difference in the overall perceived value of their education in preparing them for a job and career—some 41% of Millennials ages 25 to 32, 45% of Gen Xers and 47% of Baby Boomers say their schooling was "very useful" in getting them ready to enter the labor force. A somewhat larger share of Silents than Millennials say their education prepared them very well (50% vs. 41%).

The Value of a College Degree

Turning to college graduates, the survey finds that, regardless of their generation, adults with college degrees recognize the benefit of their undergraduate education.

---

2. According to U.S. Census Bureau data, the share of 25- to 32-year-olds with a college degree increased from 13% in 1965 to 34% in 2013.

About nine-in-ten adults with a bachelor's degree or more education (91%) say that considering what they and their family paid for their undergraduate education, it has paid off for them or they expect it will pay off in the future. The sentiment is shared by an even higher proportion (96%) of those with a graduate or professional diploma.

Those with a graduate or professional degree are the most likely to say their education was "very useful" in preparing them for the working world.

About seven-in-ten college graduates (69%) also say their undergraduate or graduate major is at least somewhat related to their current work. And few express serious regrets about their choice of college major: Only 29% say that selecting a different field of study would have better prepared them to get the kind of job they wanted.

But these views vary significantly by major, the survey found. A third (33%) of all liberal arts, social science and education majors say they should have selected another field of study to better prepare them for their ideal job. In contrast, only about a quarter (24%) of science and engineering majors express a similar regret.

As a group, those with a graduate or professional degree are the most likely to say their education was "very useful" in preparing them for the working world (69% vs. 47% for all respondents). These highly educated adults also are more likely to be very satisfied with their current job (66% vs. 52% for all) or to say they have sufficient education and training to advance in their job or career (84% vs. 59%).

Turning to demographics, Millennial college graduates are significantly less likely than older generations to currently have a job "very closely" related to their major (36% for Millennials vs. 54% for older adults).[3]

Many alumni look back on their college days fondly—but also with regrets. When it comes to better preparing themselves for the labor force, half of all college graduates say gaining more work experience while they were undergraduates would have helped their chances to get the job they wanted. Men (55%) are more likely than women (45%) to say this. About four-in-ten (38%) say that studying harder also would have improved their employment prospects—a view shared by some 47% of men but only 31% of women college graduates. As a generation, Millennials have struggled to find work during and in the aftermath of the Great Recession[4]—one likely reason that they are more likely than older adults to say more work experience in college (65% vs. 45% for older graduates) and looking for work sooner (43% vs. 26%) would have enhanced their job prospects.

The remainder of this chapter explores some of these findings in greater detail. The first section examines how those with different levels of education assess the value of their schooling in preparing them for a job and career. The next section examines whether college graduates believe their degrees were worth the money they or their families spent to send them to college. The final section explores the value of individual college degrees in the job market as well as reports what college graduates say they should have done while in school to better ready themselves for the working world.

Education and Work

The Pew Research Center survey confirms what generations of parents have told their children: To get a good job, get a good

---

3. To draw comparisions to the economic data in Chapter 1, the opening section of this chapter looked at the segment of Millennials ages 25 to 32. From this point forward, all Millennials ages 18 to 32 are included in the analysis.

4. For a detailed look at how the Great Recession affected the employment and well-being of young adults, see the Pew Resesarch Center report "Young, Underemployed and Optimistic" Feb. 9, 2012.

education. At the same time, the findings suggest that the definition of a good education has changed in recent decades, with the rewards of education disproportionately concentrated among better educated adults while those with less education are lagging far behind.

Overall about eight-in-ten adults say their education has been "very useful" (47%) or "somewhat useful" (34%) in preparing them for a job or career. Only 16% find that their education has done little or nothing to prepare them for work, the survey found.

But just beneath the overall numbers lies this striking pattern: As educational attainment increases, so do favorable judgments about the usefulness of their education in getting them ready for the labor force. In fact, these positive views rise in virtual stair-step fashion as education levels rise.

According to the survey, about seven-in-ten adults with a graduate or professional degree say their education was very useful preparing them for work, about 15 percentage points higher than those who had completed a bachelor's degree (69% vs. 55%).

The higher their level of education, the more likely an individual is to say that his or her current job is a career or a steppingstone toward a career.

The increase is nearly as large as you move up from the lower rungs of the education ladder. Some 40% of those with a high school education or less find their education very useful on the job, a proportion that increases to 49% among those with a two-year college degree.

Millennial Women More Likely than Men to See Education Useful

With one notable exception, few demographic differences exist on this question. Nearly half of all whites (45%), blacks (48%)

and Hispanics (48%) say their education was "very useful" in preparing them for a job or career. Similar shares of Millennials (46%), Gen Xers (45%) and Baby Boomers (47%) agree.

At the same time, Millennial women are more likely than either Millennial men or older men to say their education was "very useful." Among Millennials, only about four-in-ten men (39%) but 53% of women have found their education to be very beneficial in preparing them for the workforce. About half of older women (49%) and nearly as many non-Millennial men (45%) share this view.

Career and College

College is the most direct route to a good job and career. The higher their level of education, the more likely an individual is to say that his or her current job is a career or a steppingstone toward a career, a relationship that also crosses generational boundaries.

About two-thirds of all employed adults say their current job is their career (50%) or a steppingstone on the path to a career (17%). For the remaining 32%, their work is "just a job to get [them] by."

But this profile shifts dramatically by levels of education. About eight-in-ten (79%) of those with graduate or professional degrees say their current job is their career. Some 56% of those with bachelor's degrees and about an equal share (54%) of those with two-year college degrees also say they currently have a career-level position.

In contrast, only four-in-ten adults who have not graduated from college report that their current job is their career, and 15% say they are on the path to a career. The remaining 44% say their current job is just something to get them by, roughly ten times the proportion of those with a graduate degree who offer the same view.

Other Demographic Differences

The education divide is not the only significant demographic difference separating those with a career and those who are not yet there. In fact, it's not even the largest.

Large differences emerge when the focus shifts to race and ethnicity. Non-Hispanic whites (59%) are about twice as likely as blacks (29%) or Hispanics (22%) to say their current job is their career.

At the same time, Hispanics are about twice as likely as whites to say that their current job is just something to get them by (56% vs. 26%), a disparity that in part reflects educational differences between Hispanics and whites. For much the same reason, blacks also are significantly more likely than whites to be off the career path (44% vs. 26%).

More predictably, Gen Xers (58%) and Baby Boomers (59%) are significantly more likely to say they are in a career than Millennials (31%), who are just beginning their working lives. But a third of Millennials say they have their foot in the door: They are about twice as likely as Gen Xers (33% vs. 14%) and roughly five times as likely as Boomers (33% vs. 6%) to say their current job is a steppingstone to a career.

Social science, liberal arts and education majors are more likely than business majors to say they will return to school or "maybe" will go back.

But when it comes to non-career jobs, similar shares of Millennials (36%) and Boomers (34%) say their current job is just something "to get me by."

Labor economists know that income, education and employment type are closely associated. Better-educated individuals are more likely to occupy better paying jobs, which largely explains why survey respondents with annual family incomes of $100,000 or more are more than twice as likely as those making less than $50,000 to say they are in career jobs (77% vs. 31%).

At the same time, about half (49%) of those with family incomes below $50,000 say their work is just a job to get them by, a view held by only 10% of highest-earning adults.

Back to School

The value of education on the job is clearly seen when adults younger than 65 and not in school are asked if they ever plan to resume their education. A quarter say they intend to return to school someday, and an additional 11% say they might.

According to the survey, those who have not obtained a bachelor's degree are more likely than those who have at least a bachelor's degree to have plans to return to school (28% vs. 18%). Yet even people who have a four-year degree under their belt are considering going back to school, with fully 21% of bachelor's degree holders and 12% of post-graduate degree holders saying they will resume their education.

Social science, liberal arts and education majors are more likely than business majors to say they will return to school or "maybe" will go back (40% vs 23%). Some 28% of science and engineering majors say they are definitely or maybe planning to return to school.

The survey also found that blacks and Hispanics are twice as likely to say they plan to go back to school as whites. About four-in-ten (43% of blacks and 41% of Hispanics) say this, compared with 18% of whites—a relationship that holds up even accounting for different levels of education.

For example, 42% of blacks with less than a bachelor's degree and 41% of Hispanics with the same level of education intend to return to school, compared with 21% of whites with comparable education.

As might be expected, plans to return to school diminish with age. About half (54%) of 18- to 29-year-olds intend to

17

return to school. This share falls to 28% among 30- to 49-year-olds and only 10% among 50- to 64-year-olds. The question was not asked of respondents ages 65 and older.

Household income also is modestly correlated with the intent to go back to school. People in families making less than $50,000 per year are the most likely to have plans to return (33% say they will). By contrast, 18% of those in families making between $50,000 and $99,999, and 14% of those making $100,000 or more say they plan to go back to school.

As might be expected, those who think they need more training or education to succeed in their career are more likely to plan to go back to school. About four-in-ten (41%) of those currently employed who say they need more training to get ahead in their job or career intend to go back to school, compared with only 14% of those who feel they already have the necessary education. A similar share (45%) of those not employed who say they need more training in order to get the kind of job they want intend to return to school, while only 17% who already have the education they need have plans to go back.

Is College Still Worth It?

In spite of rising tuition rates at both public and private colleges, most college graduates agree that college has paid off.[5] A significant majority (83%) of bachelor's degree holders believe that they have already seen a return on what they and their family paid for their bachelor's degree. An additional 8% say that it hasn't paid off yet, but they believe it will in the future. Only 6% of graduates say that college has not paid off for them and that they do not expect it to in the future.

The generations agree that getting their college degree was worthwhile. But Gen Xers (84%) and Boomers (89%) are significantly more likely than Millennials (62%) to say they al-

5. For a detailed look at trends in college costs, see this Pew Research Center report "Is College Worth It?" May 15, 2011.

ready have seen a payoff. By contrast, for the remainder of those who say their degree has not yet paid off, Millennials are more likely than older generations to think it will eventually be worth it (26% vs. 6% for Gen Xers and 3% for Boomers.)

Majorities of college graduates say their education paid off, regardless of their family income. But college graduates with family incomes of at least $50,000 per year are more likely than those earning less to feel that their degrees have already paid off (90% vs. 63%). Those in the top income tier, earning $100,000 or more, are the most likely to say this (98%).

The Pew Research Center poll shows that the higher the degree attained, the more graduates feel their undergraduate education has paid off. Among those with postgraduate degrees, almost all have no regrets (93% say their bachelor's degree has paid off and 3% believe it will in the future).

Slightly fewer of those whose highest educational attainment is a bachelor's degree are as positive (89% say it's paid off or think it will), and even fewer—but still a sizable majority—of those with two-year college degrees say the same (76%).

Despite the higher sticker price at most private colleges, graduates from public and private schools express similar satisfaction in value for their money. Some 84% of public college graduates and 81% of private college graduates say that their education has paid off, and an additional 9% of public college graduates and 7% of private college graduates say it will pay off in the future. . . .

2

A College Degree Remains a Good Investment but Debt Is an Issue

The Domestic Policy Council and the Council of Economic Advisers

The Domestic Policy Council coordinates the domestic policy-making process in the White House, and the Council of Economic Advisers is an agency within the Executive Office of the President advising on domestic and international economic policy.

College graduates benefit from higher earnings and less unemployment than those who did not complete college, among other benefits. As college enrollment rates have increased, so has student loan debt, which most borrowers find affordable but for some it is a burden.

College continues to be an excellent investment for most students. The median annual earnings among recipients of a Bachelor's degree or higher (age 25 and over) with full-time work was $62,300 in 2013, or $28,300 more than their counterparts with only a high school diploma. College graduates also faced lower rates of unemployment than those with only a high school diploma, at 4 percent versus 8 percent. Adults with some college or a two-year degree were also better

The Domestic Policy Council and the Council of Economic Advisers, "Taking Action: Higher Education and Student Debt," The White House, June 2014, pp. 5–11. All rights reserved. Reproduced by permission.

off, but the benefits were smaller: those employed full-time earned on average $39,000 annually, $5,200 more than their counterparts with only a high school diploma.

The Benefits of a College Education

While average returns on a college education are significant, a college education is not a guarantee of a high-paying job. Although workers with a bachelor's degree are far more likely to have greater earnings, a fraction have earnings levels more common among those with only a high school diploma. For example, 12 percent of workers age 35 to 44 with a bachelor's degree had earnings under $17,500, compared to 24 percent of workers with only a high school diploma. This minority of college graduates may have faced poor economic conditions, inability to find employment in one's area of study, or personal issues such as illness.

The growth in [college] enrollment has contributed to a rapid rise in the student loan debt balance, which stood at $1.1 trillion in early 2014 compared to $250 billion in 2003.

Some studies also report other benefits associated with higher levels of education attainment beyond earnings. According to data from the College Board, college-educated adults are more likely than others to receive health insurance and pension benefits from their employers, and in general a college education leads to healthier lifestyles, reducing health care costs. Adults with higher levels of education tend to be more active citizens than others. Finally, data from both the College Board and the Brookings Institution indicate that a college education increases the chances that an adult will move up the socioeconomic ladder.

Rising Student Loan Debt

As the value of a college degree grows, enrollment rates have also increased. Nearly two-thirds of high-school graduates enrolled in college in 2013, a six percent increase from 1995. Growth in enrollment was particularly rapid in years with poor labor market conditions due to the Great Recession. Although students from low-income families are less likely to enroll in college overall, they account for most of the increase in enrollment from 1984–2008, narrowing the college attendance gap. More than half of high-school graduates from families with the lowest 20 percent of income enrolled in college in 2008, a 21 percentage point increase from 1984. This trend is providing greater opportunities for young Americans from all backgrounds, but some of that growth in enrollment—coupled with rising college costs—has fueled a greater uptake of students taking out education loans in order to finance their college education.

The growth in enrollment has contributed to a rapid rise in the student loan debt balance, which stood at $1.1 trillion in early 2014 compared to $250 billion in 2003. In fact, student loan debt is second only to mortgages among all categories of household debt. Rising tuition and fees have also driven some of this trend, with an 87 percent increase at public four-year colleges from 1999–2000 to 2012–2013.

However, some of these increases in the price of college have been offset by grants, tax benefits, and other discounts, and debt per college graduate has increased at a much more modest rate than total outstanding student debt. Goldman Sachs Research estimates that more than half of the increase in total amount of student loan debt since 1995 is due to increased enrollment and a greater share of students financing their education through loans. The trend towards more financing is driven in part by the increasing enrollment of students from low-income families.

Future changes in college costs are unlikely to lessen the debt burden. Recent trends have been compounded at many public institutions of higher education as they face declines in state appropriations, a historically large part of public higher education financing. In almost all states—including those that are now making modest increases in their higher education budgets—higher education funding remains well below prerecession levels. Compared with the 2007–08 school year, when the recession hit, and adjusted for inflation, thirty-seven states have cut funding per student by more than 20 percent, nine states have cut funding per student by more than one-third, and per-student spending in Arizona, Louisiana, and South Carolina is down by more than 40 percent since the start of the recession.

For borrowers who do default on their loans the consequences can be severe including a damaged credit rating, tax refund offset, or garnished wages.

The Affordability of Student Loan Debt

The high returns to a college education make student loan payments affordable for most borrowers. Some borrowers, however, clearly struggle to make payments and this may be particularly concerning for students just starting their careers when earnings may be relatively low or when they are still looking for work. College graduates experience the greatest earnings benefits later in their careers. For example, bachelor's degree recipients experience a 27 percent earnings increase from age 25 to age 30, compared to a 20 percent increase for high school graduates. This difference is much larger at age 45, a 76 percent increase for bachelor's degree recipients compared to a 40 percent increase for high school graduates. The typical repayment period of a student loan occurs during the earliest years despite the fact that the benefits accrue later. Coupled with the general uncertainty in labor market outcomes for individuals at any education level, paying back student debt relatively soon after college can be a challenge.

College remains an excellent investment overall. However, taking on the debt needed to complete a degree can create challenges for some students, especially for borrowers who start school but do not end up completing a degree or credential. Ten percent of borrowers entering repayment in 2012 defaulted on a loan within two years, up from 5 percent of 2003 graduates. Borrowers who drop out of college are more likely to default than those who do not, 17 percent versus 4 percent, highlighting the importance of completing a degree or program. According to data from the Department of Education, large number of defaults are actually small balance loans— with approximately 1.7 million defaulted borrowers owing $4,000 or less on their loans, many of whom may not have completed their education. These individuals are unlikely to reap the full benefits of the educational program, and some may have left their programs due to another barrier to higher earnings, such as an illness or family emergency. Earnings after graduation also vary across majors, and major choice has also been linked to default rate, although choosing a major with high average earnings does not guarantee favorable outcomes for all students. Furthermore, prospective students may not have reliable information about earnings potential when selecting a major or a program, and economic conditions specific to a given field of study may change before a student enters the labor market.

For borrowers who do default on their loans the consequences can be severe including a damaged credit rating, tax refund offset, or garnished wages. Credit ratings are a key determinant of one's ability to purchase or rent a home, open a bank account, or finance a vehicle—all important ingredients for launching a career successfully. Moreover, these blemishes on credit reports are occurring during a time when employers are increasingly relying on credit scores in the hiring process, meaning that missing payments or defaulting on student loans can impact a student's ability to pay the loans back.

Student debt burdens may have adverse effects beyond default. High monthly payments on student loans may hamper students' ability to pay other debts or cause other financial hardship. Those with more student loan debt had a higher incidence of default on credit card loans during the Great Recession, and greater student loan debt deters student borrowers from enrolling in some types of graduate programs. Furthermore, the fear of large amounts of debt may discourage prospective students from investing in higher education despite its potential benefits.

3

A College Degree Is Not a Smart Investment for Everyone

Stephanie Owen and Isabel Sawhill

Stephanie Owen is a senior research assistant and Isabel Sawhill is codirector of the Center on Children and Families at the Brookings Institution.

Although some students experience an earnings premium from obtaining a college degree, this benefit depends on a number of factors, such as school selection, financial aid, field of study, career choice, and completion of the degree. Improvements should be made to ensure that college is a smart investment for all students.

One way to estimate the value of education is to look at the increase in earnings associated with an additional year of schooling. However, correlation is not causation, and getting at the true causal effect of education on earnings is not so easy. The main problem is one of selection: if the smartest, most motivated people are both more likely to go to college and more likely to be financially successful, then the observed difference in earnings by years of education doesn't measure the true effect of college.

Stephanie Owen and Isabel Sawhill, "Should Everyone Go to College?" Center on Children and Families at Brookings Institution, *CCF Brief*, no. 50, May 2013, pp. 1–8. Brookings.edu.

Measuring the Earnings Premium

Researchers have attempted to get around this problem of causality by employing a number of clever techniques, including, for example, comparing identical twins with different levels of education. The best studies suggest that the return to an additional year of school is around 10 percent. If we apply this 10 percent rate to the median earnings of about $30,000 for a 25- to 34-year-old high school graduate working full time in 2010, this implies that a year of college increases earnings by $3,000, and four years increases them by $12,000. Notice that this amount is less than the raw differences in earnings between high school graduates and bachelor's degree holders of $15,000, but it is in the same ballpark. Similarly, the raw difference between high school graduates and associate's degree holders is about $7,000, but a return of 10% would predict the causal effect of those additional two years to be $6,000.

Social science, liberal arts and education majors are more likely than business majors to say they will return to school or "maybe" will go back.

There are other factors to consider. The cost of college matters as well: the more someone has to pay to attend, the lower the net benefit of attending. Furthermore, we have to factor in the opportunity cost of college, measured as the foregone earnings a student gives up when he or she leaves or delays entering the workforce in order to attend school. Using average earnings for 18- and 19-year-olds and 20- and 21-year-olds with high school degrees (including those working part-time or not at all), Michael Greenstone and Adam Looney of Brookings' Hamilton Project calculate an opportunity cost of $54,000 for a four-year degree.

In this brief, we take a rather narrow view of the value of a college degree, focusing on the earnings premium. However, there are many non-monetary benefits of schooling which are harder to measure but no less important. Research suggests that additional education improves overall wellbeing by affecting things like job satisfaction, health, marriage, parenting, trust, and social interaction. Additionally, there are social benefits to education, such as reduced crime rates and higher political participation. We also do not want to dismiss personal preferences, and we acknowledge that many people derive value from their careers in ways that have nothing to do with money. While beyond the scope of this piece, we do want to point out that these noneconomic factors can change the cost-benefit calculus.

As noted above, the gap in annual earnings between young high school graduates and bachelor's degree holders working full time is $15,000. What's more, the earnings premium associated with a college degree grows over a lifetime. Hamilton Project research shows that 23- to 25-year-olds with bachelor's degrees make $12,000 more than high school graduates but by age 50, the gap has grown to $46,500. When we look at lifetime earnings—the sum of earnings over a career—the total premium is $570,000 for a bachelor's degree and $170,000 for an associate's degree. Compared to the average up-front cost of four years of college (tuition plus opportunity cost) of $102,000, the Hamilton Project is not alone in arguing that investing in college provides "a tremendous return."

It is always possible to quibble over specific calculations, but it is hard to deny that, on average, the benefits of a college degree far outweigh the costs. The key phrase here is "on average." The purpose of this brief is to highlight the reasons why, for a given individual, the benefits may not outweigh the costs. We emphasize that a 17- or 18-year-old deciding whether and where to go to college should carefully consider his or her own likely path of education and career before committing a considerable amount of time and money to that degree. With tuitions rising faster than family incomes, the typical college student is now more dependent than in the past on loans, creating serious risks for the individual student and perhaps for the system as a whole, should widespread defaults occur in the future. Federal student loans now total close to $1 trillion, larger than credit card debt or auto loans and second only to mortgage debt on household balance sheets.

Variation in the Return to Education

It is easy to imagine hundreds of dimensions on which college degrees and their payoffs could differ. Ideally, we'd like to be able to look into a crystal ball and know which individual school will give the highest net benefit for a given student with her unique strengths, weaknesses, and interests. Of course, we are not able to do this. What we can do is lay out several key dimensions that seem to significantly affect the return to a college degree. These include school type, school selectivity level, school cost and financial aid, college major, later occupation, and perhaps most importantly, the probability of completing a degree.

Mark Schneider of the American Enterprise Institute (AEI) and the American Institutes for Research (AIR) used longitudinal data from the Baccalaureate and Beyond survey to calculate lifetime earnings for bachelor's earners by type of institution attended, then compared them to the lifetime earnings of high school graduates. The difference (after accounting for tuition costs and discounting to a present value) is the value of a bachelor's degree. For every type of school (categorized by whether the school was a public institution or a nonprofit private institution and by its selectivity) this value is positive, but it varies widely. People who attended the most selective private schools have a lifetime earnings premium of over $620,000 (in 2012 dollars). For those who attended a minimally selective or open admission private school, the premium is only a third of that. Schneider performed a similar exercise with campus-level data on college graduates (compiled by the online salary information company PayScale), calculating the return on investment (ROI) of a bachelor's degree. These calculations suggest that public schools tend to have higher ROIs than private schools, and more selective schools offer higher returns than less selective ones. Even within a school type and selectivity category, the variation is striking. For example, the average ROI for a competitive public school in 2010 is 9 percent, but the highest rate within this category is 12 percent while the lowest is 6 percent.

The lifetime earnings of an education or arts major working in the service sector are actually lower than the average lifetime earnings of a high school graduate.

Another important element in estimating the ROI on a college education is financial aid, which can change the expected return dramatically. For example, Vassar College is one of the most expensive schools on the 2012 list and has a relatively low annual ROI of 6%. But when you factor in its generous aid packages (nearly 60% of students receive aid, and the average amount is over $30,000), Vassar's annual ROI increases 50%, to a return of 9%.

One of the most important takeaways from the PayScale data is that not every bachelor's degree is a smart investment. After attempting to account for in-state vs. out-of-state tuition, financial aid, graduation rates, years taken to graduate, wage inflation, and selection, nearly two hundred schools on the 2012 list have negative ROIs. Students may want to think twice about attending the Savannah College of Art and Design in Georgia or Jackson State University in Mississippi. The problem is compounded if the students most likely to attend these less selective schools come from disadvantaged families.

Variation by Field of Study and Career

Even within a school, the choices a student makes about his or her field of study and later career can have a large impact on what he or she gets out of her degree. It is no coincidence that the three schools with the highest 30-year ROIs on the 2012 PayScale list—Harvey Mudd [College], Caltech [California Institute of Technology], and MIT [Massachusetts Institute of Technology]—specialize in the STEM fields: science, technology, engineering, and math. Recent analysis by the Census Bureau also shows that the lifetime earnings of workers with bachelor's degrees vary widely by college major and occupation. The highest paid major is engineering, followed by computers and math. The lowest paid major, with barely half the lifetime earnings of engineering majors, is education, followed by the arts and psychology. The highest-earning occupation category is architecture and engineering, with computers, math, and management in second place. The lowest-earning occupation for college graduates is service. According to Census's calculations, the lifetime earnings of an education or arts major working in the service sector are actually lower than the average lifetime earnings of a high school graduate.

When we dig even deeper, we see that just as not all college degrees are equal, neither are all high school diplomas. Anthony Carnevale and his colleagues at the Georgetown Center on Education and the Workforce use similar methodology to the Census calculations but disaggregate even further, estimating median lifetime earnings for all education levels by occupation. They find that 14 percent of people with a high school diploma make at least as much as those with a bachelor's degree, and 17 percent of people with a bachelor's degree make more than those with a professional degree. The authors argue that much of this finding is explained by occupation. In every occupation category, more educated workers earn more.

But, for example, someone working in a STEM job with only a high school diploma can expect to make more over a lifetime than someone with a bachelor's degree working in education, community service and arts, sales and office work, health support, blue collar jobs, or personal services. . . .

In fact, choice of major can also affect whether a college graduate can find a job at all. Another recent report from the Georgetown Center on Education and the Workforce breaks down unemployment rates by major for both recent (age 22–26) and experienced (age 30–54) college graduates in 2009–2010. People who majored in education or health have very low unemployment—even though education is one of the lowest-paying majors. Architecture graduates have particularly high unemployment, which may simply reflect the decline of the construction industry during the Great Recession. Arts majors don't fare too well, either. The expected earnings (median full-time earnings times the probability of being employed) of a young college graduate with a theater degree are about $6,000 more than the expected earnings of a young high school graduate. For a young person with a mechanical engineering degree, the expected earnings of the college graduate is a staggering $35,000 more than that of a typical high school graduate.

It is a mistake to unilaterally tell young Americans that going to college—any college—is the best decision they can make.

Variation in Graduation Rates

Comparisons of the return to college by highest degree attained include only people who actually complete college. Students who fail to obtain a degree incur some or all of the costs of a bachelor's degree without the ultimate payoff. This has major implications for inequalities of income and wealth, as the students least likely to graduate—lower-income students—are also the most likely to take on debt to finance their education.

Fewer than 60 percent of students who enter four-year schools finish within six years, and for low-income students it's even worse. Again, the variation in this measure is huge. Just within Washington, D.C., for example, six-year graduation rates range from a near-universal 93 percent at Georgetown University to a dismal 19 percent at the University of D.C. Of course, these are very different institutions, and we might expect high-achieving students at an elite school like Georgetown to have higher completion rates than at a less competitive school like UDC. In fact, Frederick Hess and his colleagues at AEI [American Enterprise Institute] have documented that the relationship between selectivity and completion is positive, echoing other work that suggests that students are more likely to succeed in and graduate from college when they attend more selective schools. At the most selective schools, 88 percent of students graduate within six years; at non-competitive schools, only 35 percent do. Furthermore, the range of completion rates is negatively correlated with school ranking, meaning the least selective schools have the widest range. For example, one non-competitive school, Arkansas Baptist College, graduates 100 percent of its students, while only 8 percent of students at Southern University at New Orleans finish. Not every student can get into Harvard, where the likelihood of graduating is 97 percent, but students can choose to attend a school with a better track record within their ability level.

Unfortunately, recent evidence by Caroline Hoxby of Stanford and Christopher Avery of Harvard shows that most high-achieving low-income students never even apply to the selective schools that they are qualified to attend—and at which they would be eligible for generous financial aid. There is clearly room for policies that do a better job of matching students to schools.

The Need for Information

All of this suggests that it is a mistake to unilaterally tell young Americans that going to college—any college—is the best decision they can make. If they choose wisely and attend a school with generous financial aid and high expected earnings, and if they don't just enroll but graduate, they can greatly improve their lifetime prospects. The information needed to make a wise decision, however, can be difficult to find and hard to interpret.

One solution is simply to make the type of information discussed above more readily available. A study by Andrew Kelly and Mark Schneider of AEI found that when parents were asked to choose between two similar public universities in their state, giving them information on the schools' graduation rates caused them to prefer the higher-performing school.

Research suggests that grants and loans increase enrollment but that aid must be tied to performance in order to affect persistence.

The PayScale college rankings are a step in the right direction, giving potential students and their parents information with which to make better decisions. Similarly, the [Barack] Obama Administration's new College Scorecard is being developed to increase transparency in the college application process. As it operates now, a prospective student can type in a college's name and learn its average net price, graduation rate, loan default rate, and median borrowed amount. The Department of Education is working to add information about the earnings of a given school's graduates. There is also a multidimensional search feature that allows users to find schools by location, size, and degrees and majors offered. The Student Right to Know Before You Go Act, sponsored by Senators Ron Wyden (D-OR) and Marco Rubio (R-FL), also aims to expand the data available on the costs and benefits of individual schools, as well as programs and majors within schools.

The College Scorecard is an admirable effort to help students and parents navigate the complicated process of choosing a college. However, it may not go far enough in improving transparency and helping students make the best possible decisions. A recent report by the Center for American Progress (CAP) showed a draft of the Scorecard to a focus group of college-bound high school students and found, among other things, that they are frequently confused about the term "net price" and give little weight to six-year graduation rates because they expect to graduate in four. It appears that the White House has responded to some of these critiques, for example showing median amount borrowed and default rates rather than the confusing "student loan repayment." Nevertheless, more information for students and their parents is needed.

The Need for Improvements

There is also room for improvement in the financial aid system, which can seem overwhelmingly complex for families not familiar with the process. Studies have shown that students frequently underestimate how much aid they are eligible for, and don't claim the tax incentives that would save them money. Since 2009, the Administration has worked to simplify the FAFSA [Free Application for Federal Student Aid], the form that families must fill out to receive federal aid—but more could be done to guide low-income families through the process.

In the longer run, colleges need to do more to ensure that their students graduate, particularly the lower-income students who struggle most with persistence and completion. Research suggests that grants and loans increase enrollment but that aid must be tied to performance in order to affect persistence. Currently, we spend over $100 billion on Pell Grants and federal loans, despite a complete lack of evidence that this money leads to higher graduation rates. Good research on programs like Georgia's HOPE scholarships or West Virginia's PROMISE scholarships suggest that attaching strings to grant aid can improve college persistence and completion.

Finally, we want to emphasize that the personal characteristics and skills of each individual are equally important. It may be that for a student with poor grades who is on the fence about enrolling in a four-year program, the most bang-for-the-buck will come from a vocationally-oriented associate's degree or career-specific technical training. Indeed, there are many well-paid job openings going unfilled because employers can't find workers with the right skills—skills that young potential workers could learn from training programs, apprenticeships, a vocational certificate, or an associate's degree. Policymakers should encourage these alternatives at the high school as well as the postsecondary level, with a focus on high-demand occupations and high-growth sectors. There has long been resistance to vocational education in American high schools, for fear that "tracking" students reinforces socioeconomic (and racial) stratification and impedes mobility. But if the default for many lower-achieving students was a career-focused training path rather than a path that involves dropping out of traditional college, their job prospects would probably improve. For example, Career Academies are high schools organized around an occupational or industry focus, and have partnerships with local employers and colleges. They have been shown by gold standard research to increase men's wages, hours worked, and employment stability after high school, particularly for those at high risk of dropping out.

4

A Four-Year College Degree Is Not Preparing People for Today's Jobs

Robert Reich

Robert Reich, the former US secretary of labor, is the Chancellor's Professor of Public Policy at the University of California at Berkeley and senior fellow at the Blum Center for Developing Economies.

College does not prepare all students for good jobs. There are many technician jobs that only require two years of technical training and community colleges could be utilized to fill this need, taking some cues from the German technical education system.

This week [September 1–5, 2014], millions of young people head to college and universities, aiming for a four-year liberal arts degree. They assume that degree is the only gateway to the American middle class.

It shouldn't be.

The Problems with College

For one thing, a four-year liberal arts degree is hugely expensive. Too many young people graduate laden with debts that take years if not decades to pay off.

And too many of them can't find good jobs when they graduate, in any event. So they have to settle for jobs that don't require four years of college. They end up overqualified for the work they do, and underwhelmed by it.

Others drop out of college because they're either unprepared or unsuited for a four-year liberal arts curriculum. When they leave, they feel like failures.

We need to open other gateways to the middle class.

Jobs That Do Not Require Four Years

Consider, for example, technician jobs. They don't require a four-year degree. But they do require mastery over a domain of technical knowledge, which can usually be obtained in two years.

Technician jobs are growing in importance. As digital equipment replaces the jobs of routine workers and lower-level professionals, technicians are needed to install, monitor, repair, test, and upgrade all the equipment.

Hospital technicians are needed to monitor ever more complex equipment that now fills medical centers; office technicians, to fix the hardware and software responsible for much of the work that used to be done by secretaries and clerks.

As our aspirations increasingly focus on four-year college degrees, we've allowed vocational and technical education to be downgraded and denigrated.

Automobile technicians are in demand to repair the software that now powers our cars; manufacturing technicians, to upgrade the numerically controlled machines and 3-D printers that have replaced assembly lines; laboratory technicians, to install and test complex equipment for measuring results; telecommunications technicians, to install, upgrade, and repair the digital systems linking us to one another.

Technology is changing so fast that knowledge about specifics can quickly become obsolete. That's why so much of what technicians learn is on the job.

But to be an effective on-the-job learner, technicians need basic knowledge of software and engineering, along the domain where the technology is applied—hospitals, offices, automobiles, manufacturing, laboratories, telecommunications, and so forth.

The Community College System

Yet America isn't educating the technicians we need. As our aspirations increasingly focus on four-year college degrees, we've allowed vocational and technical education to be downgraded and denigrated.

Still, we have a foundation to build on. Community colleges offering two-year degree programs today enroll more than half of all college and university undergraduates. Many students are in full-time jobs, taking courses at night and on weekends. Many are adults.

Community colleges are great bargains. They avoid the fancy amenities four-year liberal arts colleges need in order to lure the children of the middle class.

Even so, community colleges are being systematically starved of funds. On a per-student basis, state legislatures direct most higher-education funding to four-year colleges and universities because that's what their middle-class constituents want for their kids.

American businesses, for their part, aren't sufficiently involved in designing community college curricula and hiring their graduates, because their executives are usually the products of four-year liberal arts institutions and don't know the value of community colleges.

The German System

By contrast, Germany provides its students the alternative of a world-class technical education that's kept the German economy at the forefront of precision manufacturing and applied technology.

The skills taught are based on industry standards, and courses are designed by businesses that need the graduates. So when young Germans get their degrees, jobs are waiting for them.

We shouldn't replicate the German system in full. It usually requires students and their families to choose a technical track by age 14. "Late bloomers" can't get back on an academic track.

But we can do far better than we're doing now. One option: Combine the last year of high school with the first year of community college into a curriculum to train technicians for the new economy.

Affected industries would help design the courses and promise jobs to students who finish successfully. Late bloomers can go on to get their associate degrees and even transfer to four-year liberal arts universities.

This way we'd provide many young people who cannot or don't want to pursue a four-year degree with the fundamentals they need to succeed, creating another gateway to the middle class.

Too often in modern America, we equate "equal opportunity" with an opportunity to get a four-year liberal arts degree. It should mean an opportunity to learn what's necessary to get a good job.

5

Strengthening Our Economy Through College for All

David A. Bergeron and Carmel Martin

David A. Bergeron is senior fellow for postsecondary education at the Center for American Progress. Carmel Martin is the executive vice president for policy at the Center for American Progress.

The US economy has a growing need for college-educated workers, yet the rate of college attendance in the United States has flattened. Affordable two- or four-year college programs should be an option for all by ensuring that financial aid is available for every student who needs it.

The nation's economy demands that workers possess increasing levels of knowledge, skills, and abilities that are best acquired through postsecondary education. Without workers who have the right foundations, the United States will lose ground to countries that have prepared better for the demands of the 21st century workforce and, ultimately, the United States economy and security will be jeopardized. It is time for a new plan—what CAP calls College for All—to ensure that Americans are prepared to meet the demands of the new global economy.

On January 9, President Barack Obama announced a plan that would go a long way toward making this goal a reality by making community college free for nearly all students. In a recent report, the Commission on Inclusive Prosperity called for taking even more aggressive action to ensure that every American has access to two-year or four-year programs of postsecondary education. Under this College for All proposal, the federal government would ensure that any student attending public college or university would not be asked to pay any tuition and fees during enrollment. Students and families will not need to complete the Free Application for Federal Student Aid to receive support from the federal government. Students who achieve significant economic gains from the education they receive would repay some or all of the funds provided through the tax system.

The country has begun to lose ground on college-attainment rates as college costs have skyrocketed.

The U.S. Economy Demands Increasing Levels of Educational Attainment

A recent study by Georgetown University's Center on Education and the Workforce found that at current levels of production, the U.S. economy will have a shortfall of 5 million college-educated workers by 2020. This gap is unsurprising. By 2020, 65 percent of all jobs will require bachelor's or associate's degrees or some other education beyond high school, particularly in the fastest growing occupations—science, technology, engineering, mathematics, health care, and community service. Although the U.S. economy is demanding workers with increasing levels of education beyond high school, the postsecondary educational attainment rate has changed very little over the past decade, while other countries have made more significant gains in postsecondary educational attainment. Adults in the United States between the ages of 55 and 64 are the third most educated among the 34

Organisation for Economic Co-operation and Development, or OECD, countries that are competitors for future jobs. Meanwhile, young adults in the United States ranked 10th in terms of their rate of postsecondary education credentials among OECD peers.

Present-day 55 to 64 year-olds attained postsecondary education at a time when state and federal investment in postsecondary education was high and tuition for public colleges and universities was affordable for many middle-class families. As state investment in postsecondary education has fallen and as tuition and student-loan debt have increased, the current generation has not been able to keep up with the gains in postsecondary educational attainment achieved by many other countries. As older adults exit the workforce through retirement, U.S. economic performance will fall behind societies with higher levels of education.

The federal government has been doing its part by providing tax credits, grants to low- and moderate-income students, and loans to anyone who wants to borrow. In fiscal year 2015, these benefits are estimated to provide a total of more than $160 billion to students enrolled in postsecondary education.

If the federal government is providing this much support, why hasn't the United States seen dramatic changes in the share of the nation's adult population with postsecondary degrees and certificates? First, after making considerable gains beginning in the 1970s, the college-going rate among recent high school graduates has flattened, particularly among students from low-income families. As noted in a recent Center for American Progress report, titled "A Great Recession, a Great Retreat," the country has begun to lose ground on college-attainment rates as college costs have skyrocketed. Both the share of students borrowing to finance their education and the average amount of borrowing have increased. States have withdrawn public investment in higher education, and many students from low- and middle-income families have been priced out of public colleges and universities. This has resulted in a decline in the college-going rate among low-income students and a dramatic slowing of the rate among middle-income students.

In "A Great Recession, a Great Retreat," CAP proposed the creation of the Public College Quality Compact—a fund to encourage states to reinvest in postsecondary education. In addition to other requirements, states that wish to participate in the fund would be required to create reliable funding streams to public colleges and universities that provide at least as much as the maximum Pell Grant per student in support. Ensuring that states make reliable investments in their citizens will mean that college education is affordable for low-income students who pursue associate's or bachelor's degrees by guaranteeing grant aid to cover their enrollment at public institutions.

All high school graduates should be able to attend a public two- or four-year college or university in their home states without having to worry about whether they can afford the tuition and fees.

Affordable Higher Education Is Necessary but Not Sufficient

Making college more affordable is certainly essential. However, in order to meet short- and long-term economic needs, the higher-education system must be easier to navigate, as well as more transparent.

When students graduating from high school ask how much it will cost to go to college this year, they will likely hear "it depends." If they are fortunate, soon-to-be high school graduates will learn about the net price of attending a particular college or university by looking at the information on the Department of Education's College Navigator or College Scorecard or by looking for the net price calculators that colleges or universities are required to have on their websites. After soon-to-be graduates apply for admission, complete the Free Application for Federal Student Aid, or FAFSA, and meet other requirements, they *might* get a Financial Aid Shopping Sheet or another type of financial aid award letter that tells them how much financial aid they will receive and how much they will need to pay out of pocket or borrow. For many low- and moderate-income students, particularly those from families where the student is the first to attend college, all of this information—or the lack of specific information—fails to convey the message that college is for you and that you can afford to go.

All high school graduates should be able to attend a public two- or four-year college or university in their home states without having to worry about whether they can afford the tuition and fees. But how can graduates and their families pay for it?

Colleges and universities, even public ones, need revenue to pay faculty and staff adequate wages commensurate with their own educational attainment and professional role, build and maintain facilities, and keep the lights on. But consider this: Total tuition and fee revenues at public two- and four-year colleges totaled less than $64 billion in 2013. Included in that total was tuition and fees paid by grants and loans.

Using data from the National Center for Education Statistics' 2011–12 National Postsecondary Student Aid Survey, it is possible to estimate the net tuition and fee revenue from undergraduate students after all grants are applied. That analysis suggests that the net tuition and fee revenue received from public two- and four-year colleges and universities is substantially less. In the 2011–12 school year, two- and four-year public colleges and universities earned $58 billion in revenue from tuition and fees. But, after subtracting the grants provided, the net revenue was only $34 billion—or 59 percent of gross revenue. Among students receiving Pell Grants, the difference between the earned and net revenues was even more dramatic. Two- and four-year public colleges earned nearly $22 billion in tuition and fees from Pell Grant recipients, and they collected only $4 billion—or 19 percent of gross revenue from Pell Grant recipients. Meanwhile, community colleges collected less than $500 million—or 8 percent of gross revenue—annually in tuition and fees. It is important to note that tuition and fees do not include additional student expenses such as room and board, books, supplies, and/or transportation, otherwise referred to as cost of attendance.

Under College for All, the type of aid each student could receive would vary based on their family's long-term economic circumstance.

Replacing the net tuition and fee revenues paid by all Pell Grant recipients—or, for that matter, all undergraduates—is not outside the means or ability of the American people, particularly if this investment were made in partnership with states, as called for in "A Great Recession, a Great Retreat."

A Necessary Investment in Our Future

In 2013, the Center for American Progress convened a transatlantic Commission on Inclusive Prosperity aimed at establishing sustainable and inclusive prosperity over the long term in developed economies, with a specific focus on raising wages, expanding job growth, and ensuring broadly shared economic growth. The commission was composed of high-level American and international policymakers, economists, business leaders, and labor representatives and was charged with developing new and thoughtful solutions to spur middle-class growth.

The Report of the Commission on Inclusive Prosperity outlines an even more aggressive College for All plan to make education beyond high school universal without students or families having to come up with the funds to pay tuition and fees prior to enrolling either at a community college or a public four-year college or university in the United States. By taking such a step, all high school graduates and their families will know that they can afford higher education. College for All would provide every high school graduate financial support at a level up to the tuition and fees at a public four-year college or university. If students attend community college, they would receive an amount that would cover the cost of attendance. If a student attends a private college or university, the student would receive an amount equal to tuition and fees at the comparable public college or university in the student's home state.

Under College for All, the type of aid each student could receive would vary based on their family's long-term economic circumstance. Today, a family's income in the past full calendar year immediately prior to enrolling in college is used to determine the amount and types of federal aid a student will receive. This assessment may, or may not, bear any relationship to the long-term economic health of the student's family. Under the current system, the amount of aid provided often does not fully cover the cost, discouraging many low- and middle-income students from pursuing degrees or opting for the less expensive, lower quality options. In 2011–12, for example, students from the bottom income quintile faced average costs not met by grants and loans at public four-year colleges of nearly $6,700, or 58 percent of the average income of this group. Those at the second lowest income quintile faced costs of $7,600, or 26 percent of the average income of this group.

Students must repay much of the aid provided by the federal government, and that would continue to be true under the College for All plan. But repayment would depend on the graduate's income and would be streamlined in that there would be only one payment made through the Internal Revenue Service. The repayment terms would be more generous for low- and moderate-income students than the current 10 percent or 15 percent of discretionary income earned each year after college. Like today under the income-based student-loan repayment plans, students would be required to repay only for a specified period of time—for example, 20 years or 25 years. Former students who are struggling economically would not be required to make payments until their earnings are sufficient. And similar to the payroll tax for Social Security, there would be a cap on the amount that an individual would need to repay. Finally, aid that does not have to be repaid, such as today's Pell Grant or American Opportunity Tax Credit, would be retained but targeted at the most at-risk students at public and private colleges and universities.

Studies have suggested that the current financial aid system fails to reach its full potential because it is overly complex. Since those studies were completed, federal student aid programs have become significantly easier to access as a result of changes to the Free Application for Federal Student Aid. But it is likely still true that a radically simpler system that is easy to explain would show more robust impacts.

In the coming months, the Center for American Progress will be laying out the parameters of the new College for All proposal in a series of reports. These reports will address how an early guarantee of federal financial aid could eliminate barriers to a postsecondary education; how much the federal government would provide to cover costs at community colleges, public four-year colleges and universities, and private non-profit and for-profit colleges; how those amounts will be determined; the levels of grant support that would be provided to low- and moderate-income students; and how the repayment terms will be structured. The reports will also address how much College for All will cost taxpayers and what the return on this investment will be. The overall goal of this endeavor is to ensure that the United States has the skilled workforce and educated citizenry to achieve inclusive prosperity and economic growth. College for All is radically student-centric and will significantly increase the college-attainment among students from low- and moderate-income families.

6

The Economy Does Not Depend on Higher Education

Arthur M. Cohen, Carrie B. Kisker, and Florence B. Brawer

Arthur M. Cohen is a professor emeritus of higher education at the University of California Los Angeles and a former president of the Center for the Study of Community Colleges. Carrie B. Kisker is a consultant in education research and policy based in Los Angeles. Florence B. Brawer is a former research director of the Center for the Study of Community Colleges. This viewpoint is adapted from their book The American Community College.

The stagnant US economy is not the result of a lack of college-educated people. Rather, there is a trend toward lower-paying jobs that do not require a college education. Although a college education is desirable, it is not required for a healthy US economy.

The presumption that a shortage of educated people is responsible for a stagnant economy has been repeated frequently, especially since the onset of the recession, in 2008. A commission sponsored by the American Association of Community Colleges concluded that the nation's fiscal problems were accentuated by the fact that 59 percent of all employees needed postsecondary degrees or certificates for their jobs. In announcing the American Graduation Initiative, President Obama specified that an additional five million college graduates were needed because the nation's economy depended on the education of its workers. The Lumina Foundation has declared the imminence of an economic decline due to a gap of 23 million two- and four-year degrees by 2020.

These contentions tying the state of the economy to the number of people completing college programs are not warranted. Full-time employment declined by 5.7 million from November 2007 to November 2011, a figure that does not include the millions more who lost their jobs and gave up seeking new ones after their unemployment benefits ran out. Had all the laid-off workers somehow become unskilled and forgotten how to work? Or had their jobs been downsized, automated, or exported out from under them?

No reliable data are available showing the number of certificates or degrees needed for work-force development, unemployment reduction, or economic improvement. The oft-cited shortfall of millions of degrees is based on deceptive reasoning: Credentials are not even relevant for most jobs. For example, the great majority of jobs that were sent overseas have been filled by people less educated than the Americans they displaced. These jobs will not return until the declining salaries paid in the United States intersect with rising wages in other countries; that is, until the United States gets closer to the bottom in the worldwide race to pay the lowest wages for the same work.

Advances in productivity in other countries have not depended on significant increases in schooling.

Discouraging as such a concept may be, the trend toward lower-paying jobs is already evident. Most jobs that were lost during the recession paid mid-level wages, but the majority of positions filled in the recovery pay less. Those jobs that paid from $7.69 to $13.83 per hour accounted for 21 percent of the job losses during the recession but 58 percent of the job

growth from late 2009 through early 2012. The mid-level occupations with hourly pay of up to $21.13 accounted for 60
percent of the jobs lost but only 22 percent of the new hires.
Furthermore, this June, the Labor Department reported 2.7
million temporary workers, the highest number in history. If
they were included in the statistics, they would further depress
the salary figures.

Recently the U.S. unemployment rate dropped below 7.2
percent as thousands of workers regained their old jobs or
found new employment. In particular, residential construction
has revived, and the building industry has added 377,000 jobs
over the past two years. Legions of carpenters, electricians,
plumbers, and equipment operators have returned to work. It
is doubtful that many of them obtained postsecondary credentials while they were unemployed, nor did those who regained their jobs selling building supplies, home furnishings,
or appliances as a consequence of increased construction activity.

Advances in productivity in other countries have not depended on significant increases in schooling. For many years,
the apprenticeship systems in Japan and Northern Europe
have been popular ways of preparing the work force. Short-
term technical and vocational programs are another. Contentions that problems of international competitiveness can be
solved by increasing the years of schooling divert attention
from the corporate managers who exported the jobs origi-
nally, lobbied incessantly to avoid paying taxes on the profits
derived thereby, converted full-time positions to part-time to
avoid paying benefits, and did not invest significantly in on-
the-job training for their remaining workers.

The paucity of corporate-training and apprenticeship programs creates a niche business opportunity for postsecondary
institutions—community colleges and for-profit enterprises,
especially—to provide worker training and curricula to upgrade skills. Indeed, these occupational programs have re-

ceived $2-billion in special federal funds over the past four years and will undoubtedly contribute to the number of people holding postsecondary degrees and certificates.

At first glance, everyone wins with efforts to encourage more people to go to college, such as the College Board's College Completion Agenda, for which the goal is to have 55 percent of Americans with college degrees by 2025. Community colleges and for-profit institutions increase their enrollments, and in the latter case, profit from tuition revenues subsidized almost wholly by federal student-aid programs. Businesses gain skilled workers at little or no cost to themselves. And America's workers can add a new line or two to their résumés. But the question remains: Are all these new degrees and certificates necessary?

The high unemployment numbers are not due to workers' lacking the right education.

The data on necessary educational levels are based on variant definitions. The Current Population Survey administered by the U.S. Census Bureau classifies more than 60 percent of all jobs as postsecondary, but the Bureau of Labor Statistics reports half as many: 31 percent. This wide discrepancy is because the CPS tallies the education levels of people who are currently working in various jobs, whereas the BLS statistics reflect the entry-level education requirements for those jobs (a classification that seems to change from year to year). Thus, the job held by a college-educated barista would be classified as postsecondary by the CPS but not by the BLS. Obviously, jobs data that trace the degrees held by current employees are subject to distorted interpretation.

The Economic Policy Institute's review of job data shows that 52 percent of employed college graduates under the age of 24 are working in jobs that don't require college degrees. Put another way, of the 21 million workers earning less than

$10.01 per hour, 3.57 million hold college degrees and an additional 5.46 million have some college. That these sales representatives, clerks, cashiers, and restaurant servers hold associate or bachelor's degrees does not mean they needed to present them when they applied.

Certainly higher education is desirable. The community gains people more likely to be charitable, to vote, and to participate in civic affairs, and less likely to rely on governmental assistance or engage in antisocial behavior. The individual learns to reason scientifically and think critically and gains a sense of historical perspective, an appreciation for aesthetics and cultural diversity, and access to training for the professions that require credentials.

The notion that a person without a degree is doomed to unemployment is at best a widespread misconception, as unwarranted as blaming an economic recession on a paucity of skilled workers. The high unemployment numbers are not due to workers' lacking the right education. The numbers reflect the weak demand for goods and services, a weakness that makes it unnecessary for employers to hire workers at any level of education.

Yet, sustained by the mutuality of interests between college educators who embrace the jobs attendant on high enrollments and the business leaders who profit from having their employees prepared at public expense, the misrepresentation persists. The statement "By the year 2018, all jobs will require a higher education," which comes from a report called "Help Wanted," by the Center on Education and the Workforce at Georgetown University, has become so commonplace that a version recently appeared as an advertisement on the rear of buses in Los Angeles. The sponsor? A local nonprofit group promoting its chain of preschools. Nobody would argue that greater access to education is a bad thing—especially for the preschool set—but the motives of those promoting these statements, as well as those who uncritically accept them out of self-interest, are open to question.

7

There Are Economic Benefits from Obtaining a College Degree

Jonathan Rothwell

Jonathan Rothwell is a senior research associate and an associate fellow in the Metropolitan Policy Program at the Brookings Institution.

A college education delivers economic benefits not only to the US economy but to the individual. The manufacturing sector illustrates the change in recent years from jobs that did not need a college education to those that do, particularly in science, technology, engineering, and mathematics—the so-called STEM occupations.

In the face of ever-rising tuition and scarce or confusing quality metrics, many people are understandably frustrated with universities and community colleges. Meanwhile, the Great Recession has delayed or diverted the ambitions of many young college graduates.

An Unwarranted Claim

Unfortunately, some scholars have piled on to these concerns with unwarranted suggestions that there is little to no private or public economic benefit from obtaining a college degree.

In a commentary in the *Chronicle of Higher Education*, Arthur M. Cohen, Carrie B. Kisker, and Florence B. Brawer argue that the vibrancy and productivity of the economy is unrelated to higher education. At the personal level, they imply that the likelihood of finding a job is largely unrelated to education. At the aggregate level, they deny that education benefits the economy, relegating its advantages to social and culture benefits. Therefore, they conclude, efforts to increase educational attainment should be dismissed as selfish gestures by parties that stand to gain financially—like universities and philanthropic charities dedicated to education.

Almost every year breaks a new record in the earning differences between high school and college educated workers.

These claims are contradicted by reality. The data are very clear that the sacrifices made by millions of taxpayers, parents, and individuals to invest in the education of others or themselves are economically worthwhile, as my Brookings [Institution] colleagues have pointed out.

The Economic Benefits of College

First of all, it is indisputable that workers with more education typically earn significantly higher wages and are far more likely to be employed than workers who have no post-secondary education. For example, the latest figures from the Bureau of Labor Statistics show that workers with only a high school education are twice as likely to be unemployed as those with at least a bachelor's degree. Among the employed, the median college educated worker earns 84 percent more than the median worker with only a high school education. Even those with just some college and no degree or an associate's degree earn 16 percent more. College educated workers are also much more likely to be in the labor force.

A large body of economic literature shows that these differences are not the result of a special group of very smart people getting educated. An identical twin raised in the same family but with more education earns significantly more than his or her less educated sibling. This and other evidence prove that education has an important causal effect on earnings for all groups of people.

From a longer-term perspective, the absolute and relative wage benefits of post-secondary education have steadily increased since 1980, as economists have long noted. Almost every year breaks a new record in the earning differences between high school and college educated workers. As a leading labor economist, Philip Orepoulos, and his co-author recently summarized:

> For the past three decades, technological change has led to increased growth in the demand for skilled workers, and because the supply of college educated workers has not increased at the same rate, employers have bid up the wages of college graduates causing the rise in the college earnings premium.

The Manufacturing Sector

To see how this plays out, consider the manufacturing sector. Everyone knows the number of manufacturing jobs in the United States has plummeted in recent decades. What is less well known is that the losses are concentrated among less-than-college-educated workers. From 1980 to 2013, workers with no college have seen a net loss of 9.3 million jobs in the manufacturing sector. But workers with at least some college have seen a net *increase* of 2.5 million manufacturing jobs.

How did this happen? As millions of non-college educated workers from post-communist China and other undeveloped countries moved out of subsistence farming into higher paying and more productive routine factory work, it no longer made sense to employ low-skilled American workers to do these tasks. Thus, the U.S. manufacturing sector has rapidly up-skilled both in terms of education and the skill level of occupations. These and other trends create opportunities for blue collar workers in skilled STEM [science, technology, engineering, and mathematics] fields but most need at least some post-secondary training. As scholars have found, this sort of technician training, typically found at community colleges, generates skills that make factories more efficient and valuable innovations more likely.

Those who most directly impact economic growth—inventors and entrepreneurs—also tend to be highly educated. A Georgia Tech survey of patent inventors found that 92 percent had a bachelor's degree, almost exclusively in STEM (Science, Technology, Engineering, and Mathematics) subjects. Likewise, almost all of the founders (92 percent) of the high-tech companies that have powered GDP [gross domestic product] in recent decades are college educated, especially in STEM fields. Thus, it is no surprise that macroeconomic research finds very large gains from education on economic growth at both the international and regional levels, as the research of Harvard's Ed Glaeser and many others has shown.

In their efforts to boost American education, the president, civic and political leaders of various partisan persuasions, philanthropic and religious groups, educators, parents, and many others are providing a great service to this country. They deserve our respect and our engagement to insure that they are focusing their efforts on the interventions that will most advance their goals.

8

The Value of a College Degree Is Diminishing Over Time

Richard Vedder, Christopher Denhart, and Jonathan Robe

Richard Vedder directs the Center for College Affordability and Productivity (CCAP), is a Distinguished Professor of Economics Emeritus at Ohio University, and is an adjunct scholar at the American Enterprise Institute. Christopher Denhart is a project management consultant and Jonathan Robe is a law student.

There is an underemployment problem, with college graduates performing jobs for which they are overqualified. But there is also an overinvestment problem, with society placing too many resources into a college education system that is shielded from market forces. The confluence of these forces suggests that the value of a college education is diminishing over time.

The mismatch between the educational requirements for various occupations and the amount of education obtained by workers is large and growing significantly over time. The problem can be viewed two ways. In one sense, we have an "underemployment" problem: College graduates are underemployed, performing jobs which require vastly less educational tools than they possess. The flip side of that, though, is that we have an "overinvestment" problem: We are churning out far more college graduates than required by labor-market imperatives. The supply of jobs requiring college degrees is growing more slowly than the supply of those holding such degrees. Hence, more and more college graduates are crowding out high-school graduates in such blue-collar, low-skilled jobs as taxi driver, firefighter, and retail sales clerks. Credential inflation is pervasive. And, as [Richard] Hernstein and [Charles] Murray noted nearly two decades ago, one by-product of this phenomenon is a dumbing down of the college curriculum; as they put it "credentialism . . . is part of the problem, not the solution."

The Wisdom of College for All

That suggests the earnings advantage associated with a bachelor's degree will change over time. By one way of looking at it, the college degree becomes less worthwhile financially: If one compares earnings of those with bachelor's degrees with that of all workers (not merely high-school graduates), the day may come when the bachelor's degree will pay less than that of all workers, as the proportion of workers with more than bachelor's degrees comes close to approximating that of those with less than a four-year diploma. The college degree will be the new normal, and the credential inflation leading to more and more college-educated taxi drivers will continue to escalate. Yet this is not to say going to college is unnecessary: Indeed, it would be almost impossible to get a job without a degree. Vocational success would require even more education.

Enrollments will fall, and in time the rate of return on college investments will increase again as the labor-market disconnect problem is reduced.

But at what cost? Can we afford to expend $100,000 or more in resources giving kids a college degree, only to see them take taxi driver jobs for which the college education added hardly a scintilla of employment skill? Can we afford to lose the labor services of 18-to-22 year olds going to college for little employment advantages, persons who could start driving a taxi or working as a bank teller at 18 instead of 22? In an era where the worker-to-dependent ratio is rapidly falling, the underemployed college graduate is an expensive luxury we can ill afford as a nation. To be sure, given wide variations in earnings by college attended and by major, generalizations are dangerous, and maybe some forms of college training and some institutions deserve greater support than others. Besides, it is not as if reducing societal investment in higher education would *necessarily* adversely affect national output; as [education writer and consultant] Paul Barton observes, despite the handwringing in the past about an emerging shortage of highly educated workers in the U.S., "since 1995, productivity has accelerated, with no demonstrable improvement in workforce skills or acceleration in job requirements during the period."

All of this calls into question the wisdom of the "college for all" movement. Does it make sense to become the world's leader again in the proportion of young adults with college degrees? Is the goal of individuals like President [Barack] Obama or groups like the Lumina Foundation to increase college degree attainment desirable? Should we look for new and cheaper ways to assure employee competency? Should we invest less in four-year degree programs and more in cheaper training, including high-school vocational education that once was fashionable? Perhaps the federal government should reduce its involvement in the higher-education business, much like some states seem to be starting to do out of fiscal imperatives imposed by balanced-budget requirements that the federal government does not face. If fewer students could get Pell Grants or subsidized student loans, enrollments might very well fall, an outcome we perceive not to be a bad thing from a labor-market perspective.

A Shielded Overinvestment

That raises questions that go beyond higher education. As the number of years of education of workers rises in virtually all non-professional and technical jobs, is the reason ultimately that really it takes, say, 14 or 15 years of schooling to offer the same learning that previously was accomplished in 12 years? Is the deterioration in the quality of our primary and secondary education a contributing factor in the credential inflation obvious at the postsecondary level? That suggests there may be two major economic issues facing higher education. First, it is too costly, too inefficient, too shielded from the useful market forces of "creative destruction." Second, because of massive overinvestment reflecting indifference to labor-market realities, we are vastly wasting scarce resources, both public and private.

To be sure, *if left alone*, market forces will likely solve the problem. Reading stories of underemployed college graduates with massive debt, more will start rejecting the mantra that everyone should go to college. Enrollments will fall, and in time the rate of return on college investments will increase again as the labor-market disconnect problem is reduced. There are already signs that is beginning to happen. The *Wall Street Journal* recently proclaimed, "demand for four-year college degrees is softening." Yet public policies such as massive federal loan subsidies often distort outcomes and prevent a stable and economically effective equilibrium position from being reached. As someone once joked, "when we see light at the end of the tunnel, the government adds more tunnel."

A decade ago, while contemplating calls in Britain for increased public investment in education (rhetoric that is very similar, if not identical, to the rhetoric today in the United States), the British educator Alison Wolf perceptively opined,

> Education is big because it is seen as the engine for economic growth, a sure-fire route to future prosperity and victory in a global competition . . . the belief in education for

growth runs deep and wide beyond our political classes, replacing socialism as the great secular faith of our age.

Economists for generations have long accepted the law of diminishing returns—when one adds more and more resources, at some point the marginal contribution to output falls. The law applies to education as to almost everything in life. One manifestation of it in American university life is the underemployment of college graduates; we might be seriously overinvested in higher education. This study adds to that concern, and further suggests the common assumption that increased investment in higher education promotes economic growth is highly questionable.

9

National Security and Prosperity Depend on Greater College Completion

Jamie Merisotis

Jamie Merisotis is president and chief executive officer of the Lumina Foundation, a private foundation committed to enrolling and graduating more students from college.

The United States is falling behind other countries in postsecondary education attainment, and although progress has been made in recent years, it is not moving fast enough. Education attainment beyond high school needs to grow from 40 percent today to 60 percent by 2025 for the United States to remain competitive in the global economy.

As postsecondary skills have become essential to success for millions of Americans, few would argue that our nation has all of the talent it needs to prosper. New data reveal that our country risks falling behind in a global race—the competition for innovation and, above all else, talent—unless actions are taken now to significantly increase postsecondary attainment.

Progress on Educational Attainment

Projections by the Georgetown Center on Education and the Workforce show that more than 65 percent of U.S. jobs will require some form of postsecondary education by the end of this decade. And yet, according to Lumina Foundation's just-released annual *Stronger Nation* report on postsecondary attainment rates across America, only 40 percent of working-age adults (ages 25–64) now hold at least a two-year degree.

Results from the last five years show that progress on educational attainment has been real—between 2008 and 2013, the percentage of Americans with at least a two-year degree grew by 2.1 percentage points, representing more than 2.8 million more degrees.

This progress reflects both increasing demand for postsecondary credentials and the efforts of higher education institutions, policymakers and many others to respond to that demand. And yet we must do significantly better if we intend to grow our economy, meet the labor needs of our employers, strengthen our democracy and provide opportunity to individuals across the country.

It's clear that the only way to meet our growing need for talent is to significantly increase education attainment beyond high school. Specifically, we need to reach Goal 2025—an ambitious objective for 60 percent of all Americans to have a high-quality postsecondary degree, certificate or other credential by the year 2025. And time is of the essence.

All who have a stake in the success of the American student need to join forces to really get the attainment needle moving in America.

The Demographics of College Graduates

A new urgency is needed for the sake of all Americans, not just those born into certain families or neighborhoods or income brackets. Data from the *Stronger Nation* report show persistent and widening degree attainment gaps linked to race and ethnicity.

Asian adults lead all races with 60.0 percent degree attainment; whites follow at 44.5 percent; African Americans rank a distant third at 28.1 percent; Native Americans are at 23.9 percent; and Hispanics rank fifth at 20.3 percent.

Adding to the challenge of increasing attainment is the fact that enrollment was down last year [2014]—perhaps not surprising given historic patterns following a recession, but troubling nonetheless given the urgency of achieving the 60 percent goal.

The Actions That Are Needed

Policymakers, employers, civic champions, education leaders and all who have a stake in the success of the American student need to join forces to really get the attainment needle moving in America. Here are the areas where action is most needed:

- Increasing persistence and completion. Far too many students drop out of college without completing a degree, and states and institutions need to follow the lead of states like Tennessee by implementing a comprehensive approach to increasing completion. Making college affordable for all Americans who need it should be an urgent national priority, and will require that we rethink many of our assumptions about how much college costs and how we pay for it. We also must work on creating better pathways to guide students successfully through postsecondary education systems.

- Targeting adults with "some college, no degree." As a result of attrition rates, an astounding 36.2 million Americans—nearly 22 percent of the working-age population between the ages of 25 and 64—have attended college but did not obtain a degree. All states should follow the lead of states like Georgia, Oklahoma, and Kentucky to reengage this critical group. If just 15 percent of these "some college, no degree" adults complete, that would result in nearly 5.5 million more Americans with degrees.

- Recognizing all forms of learning. For now, attainment numbers focus on Americans with degrees. But as workforce demands shift, many employers see tremendous value in hiring candidates who hold the high-quality certificates, certifications and other credentials that lead to employment and further education. It's estimated that 7.8 million Americans fall into this category. We believe that we should find ways to recognize the learning that these high-quality postsecondary credentials represent and create stronger pathways from them to degrees. Current data don't allow us to do that, but we are optimistic that improvements in data systems will soon make this possible.

For many decades, education has proven to be this nation's single most powerful engine of individual progress and upward mobility. And in today's rapidly changing workplace, that's truer than ever.

As a nation, we must work to assure not just individual opportunity but national security and prosperity as well. Since postsecondary attainment is now the key to both, social justice also requires that we make substantial progress in expanding postsecondary opportunity and closing gaps in attainment. We have 10 years to reach Goal 2025. The clock is ticking.

10

A College Education Is a Right, Not an Investment

Mario Goetz

Mario Goetz has a Residency in Social Enterprise (RISE) at the New Sector Alliance, an organization that provides fellowships to support work in the social sector.

The current cultural definition of a college education as an investment is a new idea, and it needs to be rejected. Higher education was intended to be a right and a public good that is accessible to all, and that vision needs to be renewed so that all Americans can benefit from a college education.

Tuition wasn't always so high, student loans didn't always have those interest rates, and the public higher education system could still return to its roots in social mobility and inclusion.

For many Millennials, the present higher education system exudes an overwhelming sense of permanence. In our short lives, college tuition has always been high, education funding has always been decreasing, and college has always meant a risky "investment in our futures." We know that these yearly tuition hikes are wrong, and that the current tuition rates already saddle us with debt we probably won't pay off until we retire, if we retire. For many of us, the consequences are much more immediate, as many low-income students cannot afford higher education anymore. Yet we continue to shell out the money, or take out the loans. Confronted with the institutional power of the higher education system, we feel powerless.

College as a Right and Public Good

Depressing, right? But history shows us that all is not lost by exposing the mechanisms that brought about the status quo. In their Fall 2012 article in *Dissent*, Aaron Bady and Roosevelt Institute Fellow Mike Konczal reveal what higher education used to mean and how it was systematically destroyed. Bady and Konczal transport us to 1950s–'60s California, where bipartisan support for a University of California system built the state into a land of prosperity and innovation, a burgeoning middle class sent its children to college *for free*, and progressive Republicans happily funded education to support inclusion and social mobility for California's next generation. In 1960, the Donahoe Act, or the Master Plan for Higher Education, represented California's commitment to educate anyone who wanted to be educated. Despite the concurrent trends of racism, sexism, and American imperialism that pervaded that era, California's higher education system was a golden example of what America could achieve.

The all-powerful system [of higher education] we inherited is not permanent.

So what happened? Where did it go? In 1966, Ronald Reagan was elected Governor of California and began dismantling the promising work of the past 20 years. Previously, admission had been free, except for a few relatively small fees, but the Reagan government lifted regulations on how much schools could charge in fees, allowing costs to skyrocket. Also, incentives were created for colleges to accept out-of-state students, who would pay higher fees. Both of these strategies shifted the financial responsibility for higher education onto students rather than the state. The process of culturally redefining higher education as not a right, or a public good, but an investment, subject to the whims of the marketplace and corporate capitalism, had begun.

Reagan's policies continued to affect Californian higher education after he left office. Bady and Konczal point out two of the most important elements of his legacy: Proposition 13, which cut property taxes and capped their growth rate, limiting state property tax revenue; and the prison-building boom. These policies not only decreased the amount of money the state could use to fund higher education, but also diverted a greater portion away to build prisons. Since then, state investment in higher education has decreased dramatically. Such cuts in spending came as demand for higher education continued to rise, driving up costs even further and restricting access.

Redefining College as an Investment

This conservative rethinking of higher education did not stay in California. The destruction of public education in California was the first domino in the Reagan revolution, reflected in Reagan's policies as president and in the policies of governors in other states. Bady and Konczal appropriately call California policies "the beginning of the end of public higher education in the United States as we'd known it."

These policies were the first cells of a virus that grew and replicated so effectively that it eventually posed as the institutional normal. Today, it can be hard to see through the elaborate and restrictive veil that separates us from our education. However, by understanding how it all began, we can see that the all-powerful system we inherited is not permanent. By identifying how it started, we can condemn it and clear a path toward restoring our values and our institutions.

Higher education was never meant to be an "investment." It was meant to be a public good—a right. Pursuing dreams of a college education should not require dire consequences that threaten to cancel out its benefits. Progressives and Millennials will not continue to absorb the seemingly incremental infringements on our rights and liberties. We understand history. We understand that the system was not and is not forever. Today, students fight increases in student loan interest rates, challenging the institutions that say the higher interest rates are necessary. We can take back higher education for ourselves: fight to decrease tuition and fees, increase access for all, and make higher education something we can truly be proud of as Americans.

11

There Should Be Alternatives to the Four-Year College Degree

Diana G. Carew

Diana G. Carew is director of the Young American Prosperity Project at the Progressive Policy Institute.

A college degree is only valuable because a high school diploma is worth so little. The current system saddles students with debt and harms college dropouts. These failings could be remedied by making college only one of several pathways to work and a successful career.

C ollege has never been worth so much—or so little.

The Reality of College Worth

New research from the Pew [Research] Center shows the wage gap between those with a college degree and those without is at an all-time high. Moreover, the college wage premium has actually been widening. Yet at the same time, real average earnings for young college graduates are at historic lows—down 6 percent from 2007 levels, even as the labor market recovers. Average student debt per borrower has climbed to a staggering $29,400.

Diana G. Carew, "College—Worth It or Worth Less?" *The Progressive Fix* (blog), March 26, 2014. ProgressivePolicy.org. Copyright © 2014 Diana G. Carew. All rights reserved. Reproduced by permission.

Does this double-sided truth about the "value" of college mean that today's four-year model is sustainable, or is it a sign that change is coming?

At first blush, one might conclude that going to college—specifically a four-year college—is a necessity. But that misses the point of what's actually driving the wage gap between college and non-college grads, something that young college graduates already know—that not all of this boost is because of a lift-off in the bachelor's degree job market.

The large share of college drop-outs is evidence that the current structure of postsecondary education as the main vehicle for workforce preparation isn't working.

In reality, a college degree is worth "more" in large part because a high school diploma is worth so much less. My research shows college graduates, particularly recent graduates, are increasingly taking lower-skill jobs at the expense of their less educated peers. Because many new jobs being created are low-skill instead of middle-skill, college graduates are getting first dibs, squeezing those with less education from the workforce.

The Failings of the Current System

Even worse, the price to compete for these lower-skill jobs is getting higher. As college becomes less affordable, and the labor market less generous, fewer people are able to buy the seemingly only ticket in town for success. New Fed [Federal Reserve] data shows outstanding student debt increased $53 billion in the last 3 months of 2013 alone, with student loans dominating all new borrowing by young Americans under 30 in 2013. Succeeding in today's higher education model allows for little margin of error: either you make the sacrifice and get the four year degree, or it's game over.

No group epitomizes the failings of the current college system more than those who enrolled in college but failed to graduate—college drop-outs. Though often left out of the conversation, the latest figures show that the average four-year completion rate for those entering four-year colleges was 38.6 percent and that the six-year completion rate is still just 58.8 percent (rates are lower for two-year schools, but many transfer to other institutions). Minorities and low-income Americans are even less likely to complete college, exacerbating already growing inequality.

College drop-outs face the worst struggle of all. On average, they make little more than those with a high school diploma but are still saddled with thousands in student debt. They are at the highest risk of defaulting on their student loans, by some estimates up to four times more likely than graduates. They are the most vulnerable in terms of financial security, from slipping into a hole they cannot climb out of. The large share of college drop-outs is evidence that the current structure of postsecondary education as the main vehicle for workforce preparation isn't working.

College as One of Several Options

Their fate is also an indication that the future of college may—and should—look very different. The ongoing revolution of low-cost, high speed broadband makes education more accessible, affordable, and customizable. This, coupled with decreasing returns on the four-year college model, should lead to more post-secondary pathways into the workforce (such as German-style "apprenticeships"). These alternative pathways have the potential to be just as effective at preparing people for the world of work, except at a lower cost. The nature of today's innovative data-driven economy means preparing for tomorrow's high-skill, high-wage jobs will naturally include digitally-oriented training and a dynamic curriculum.

The ideal post-secondary system of the future should correct some of the biggest workforce challenges facing Americans today. These are Americans who are unable to afford college, or who don't want to take on thousands in student debt to succeed.

One way this could happen is if the current four-year model of college becomes one of several options after high school. Instead, what we could see is employers becoming better integrated into the workforce preparation process, as current workforce demands are unmet and training becomes a lower cost proposition that can be virtually administered. We may also see a renaissance in vocational training, which can cost-effectively prepare workers for well-paid technical and even computer and data-driven jobs. Industry certifications could take the place of a degree. It may be that only a few will pursue a four-year degree, much like a doctorate-level credential is pursued today, in specialty fields.

Still, wholesale change is unlikely to happen quickly, so long as the generous federal student aid system in place prolongs the current college model. The federal government administers more than 90 percent of new student aid—to the tune of more than $100 billion annually—but demands little accountability on the part of institutions and borrowers in terms of graduation rates and employment success.

For the millions of young Americans who've already been left behind, reform can't come soon enough. That's why the conversation to rethink college must begin now.

12

College Diplomas Are Meaningless. This Is How to Fix Them

Reid Hoffman

Reid Hoffman is cofounder and executive chairman of LinkedIn, a partner at the Silicon Valley venture capital firm Greylock, and coauthor of the book The Start-up of You.

The current reliance on a four-year college degree as one of the main job screening tools fails to fully utilize modern innovations in technology. The college diploma ought to be replaced with a system of certification as a platform, using technology not only for instruction but also for certification.

Every year, millions of Americans embark on the quest to earn a four-year college degree. Many motives propel them. They go to acquire skills and knowledge from experts in their fields. They go, more generally, to learn how to learn, and to broaden their minds in ways that will help them function as autonomous adults participating fully in the civic life of their country. They go to find friends and mentors. They go because they know that in today's highly competitive job market, many employers won't even grant them an interview for a position as a receptionist or a file clerk unless they have a four-year-degree.

College marketing literature rarely expresses this last fact so bluntly. Instead, it tends to emphasize vibrant communities of scholarship and learning, stimulating atmospheres of intellectual inquiry, enduring commitments to academic excellence.

Now, however, there are an expanding number of ways to acquire specific skills and knowledge faster and less expensively than one can manage through a traditional four-year degree program. There are increasing opportunities and venues where people can seek mentorship and develop strategic alliances.

If we truly want to retool higher education for the 21st century in the most forward-thinking way possible, we shouldn't confine our retooling efforts to instruction alone.

The sole unique feature of a few thousand U.S. institutions of higher learning is their ability to grant four-year degrees. And because a diploma from a four-year program is the mechanism a majority of employers use to screen potential hires, it's both increasingly valuable and increasingly costly to obtain.

These days, getting that sheepskin from a top-flight university can cost approximately $200,000 in tuition alone. And while many schools have begun to steeply discount their advertised tuitions as they scramble to attract new students in the current market, thousands of graduates continue to emerge from college saddled with six-figure debts. In 2010, the nation's collective student loan debt exceeded its collective credit card debt for the first time in history.

To help temper the high cost of college, a number of high-tech start-ups have been making impressive strides in the realm of online instruction. But if we truly want to retool higher education for the 21st century in the most forward-thinking way possible, we shouldn't confine our retooling efforts to instruction alone.

In the same way that trailblazers like Coursera and Udacity are making instruction faster, cheaper, and more effective, we should also make certification faster, cheaper, and more effective too.

To do this, we need to apply new technologies to the primary tool of traditional certification, the diploma. We need to take what now exists as a dumb, static document and turn it into a richer, updateable, more connected record of a person's skills, expertise, and experience. And then we need to take that record and make it part of a fully networked certification platform.

Once we make this leap, certification can play a more active role in helping the higher education system clearly convey to students what skills and competencies they should pursue if their primary objective is to optimize their economic futures.

Granted college isn't just for training your people for the world of work. But if we truly believe that a college education is the best path toward general prosperity and personal fulfillment, we need to do more to ensure that our college graduates are economically viable.

One way to accomplish this is to establish certification as a platform in which the roles and interests of key players in the higher education system—students, educators, and employers—are explicitly articulated and tightly integrated. Functioning as a feedback loop, certification can then help achieve a goal that is at least as crucial as controlling tuition costs: Helping individuals stay employable and competitive in a professional landscape where the desired skills and competencies change rapidly.

Diplomas: Time for an Upgrade

We sometimes call a diploma a "sheepskin." Why? Because until around a hundred years ago, that's what most of them were made from. Then, paper diplomas began to appear. After centuries of usage, that was the big upgrade to this technology. And there really haven't been any since.

A diploma is essentially a communications device that signals a person's readiness for certain jobs. But unfortunately it's a dumb, static communication device with roots in the 12th century.

Typically, we don't think of diplomas as a "technology." But they are. Economists often speak of their "signalling" value. Equipped with a diploma, a job-seeker broadcasts numerous positive attributes to potential employers: Perseverance, self-governance, competence in at least one area.

Employers, in turn, use diplomas as screening mechanisms. If you don't have a diploma, you don't get an interview. According to the *New York Times*, even employers looking for receptionists and file clerks require a bachelor's degree these days. "When you get 800 résumés for every job ad, you need to weed them out somehow," an executive recruiter told the newspaper.

So a diploma is essentially a communications device that signals a person's readiness for certain jobs.

But unfortunately it's a dumb, static communication device with roots in the 12th century.

That needs to change.

At my alma mater, Stanford University, a bachelor's degree currently costs more than $160,000 in tuition alone. Less than ten miles from Stanford, however, another school, Foothill College, also issues degrees. There, you can get a two-year associate's degree for around $2,790, or less than 2 percent of what you'd pay for a Stanford degree.

The problem is if the baseline requirement to obtain a job interview, even for positions like "receptionist" and "file clerk," is a four-year bachelor's degree, then in practical terms an associate's degree is not even worth 2 percent of a Stanford degree. It's worth zero.

So despite the fact that colleges and other education providers have established a variety of alternative programs and degree options, at a variety of different price points, employers have simply placed more and more emphasis on traditional four-year degrees.

Not that this means employers are satisfied with the system.

In March 2013, the radio show *Marketplace* teamed up with *The Chronicle of Higher Education* and asked around 700 employers to grade the nation's colleges and universities on how well they were employing their graduates for the workplace.

The more employers realize that four-year degrees don't necessarily guarantee the attributes they value most, the more likely they'll be to demand a system that does.

---

53 percent of them said they "had trouble finding recent graduates qualified to fill positions at their company or organization." 28 percent said colleges did only a "fair job" of producing successful employees. They also said that more than grades, major, or what school a person attended, "employers viewed an internship as the single most important credential for recent grads."

At first glance, this perspective is baffling. Employers insist that college degrees are a prerequisite for employment, even for low-skilled clerical positions. And yet what they find most telling is not how well people do in four-year-degree programs, but how well they do in settings that approximate workplaces.

Thus, there's actually reason for hope here. The more employers realize that four-year degrees don't necessarily guarantee the attributes they value most, the more likely they'll be to demand a system that does.

Design Specs for a Smarter Diploma

We spend years of our lives working to obtain a diploma. We invest substantial capital in it. And yet compared to the nuanced portraits of our aptitudes and attitudes that our teachers presented to our parents on our first-grade report cards, a college diploma is an opaque and unrevealing document.

If we were building a higher education system from scratch, would our records of assessment and certification look anything like today's diplomas? Ask a hundred people to build a better diploma, and you'll probably end up with a hundred different solutions. None, however, would look like a traditional sheepskin.

In my opinion, these are the characteristics a 21ˢᵗ century diploma should have:

- It should accommodate a completely unbundled approach to education, allowing students to easily apply credits obtained from a wide range of sources, including internships, peer to peer learning, online classes, and more, to the same certification.

- It should be dynamic and upgradeable, so individuals can add new credentials to it as they pursue new goals and educational opportunities and so that the underlying system itself is improvable.

- It should help reduce the costs of higher education and increase overall value.

- It should allow a person to convey the full scope of his or her skills and expertise with greater comprehensiveness and nuance, in part to enable better matching with jobs.

- It should be machine-readable and discoverable, so employers can easily evaluate it in numerous ways as part of a larger "certification platform."

Two hundred years ago, what you learned about Latin, the Bible, and mathematics when you were 21 was just as likely to be true when you turned 70. So you spent four straight years in college lecture halls and libraries, you acquired skills and knowledge that would serve you for life, and then you were done.

Now, in today's fast-changing world, it makes more sense to learn provisionally, opportunistically, as new challenges and necessities arise.

To make this style of learning more practical, we need certification for it that employers will grow to trust and value even more than they do traditional bachelor's degrees because the efficacy will be so much better.

Imagine an online document that's iterative like a LinkedIn profile (and might even be part of the LinkedIn profile), but is administered by some master service that verifies the authenticity of its components. While you'd be the creator and primary keeper of this profile, you wouldn't actually be able to add certifications yourself. Instead, this master service would do so, verifying information with the certification issuers, at your request, after you successfully completed a given curriculum.

[In] a more modularized system . . . students could make smaller investments—in money and time—to acquire specific credentials.

Over time, this dynamic, networked diploma will contain an increasing number of icons or badges symbolizing specific certifications. It could also link to transcripts, test scores, and work examples from these curricula, and even evaluations from instructors, classmates, internship supervisors, and others who have interacted with you in your educational pursuits.

Ultimately the various certificates you earn could be bundled into higher-value certifications. If you earn five certificates in the realm of computer science, you might receive an icon or badge that symbolizes this higher level of experience and expertise. In this way, you could eventually assemble portfolios that reflect a similar breadth of experiences that you get when you pursue a traditional four-year degree.

For students, the more modularized approach to instruction embodied in such diplomas would have immediate benefits. Traditional four-year degrees maximize tuition costs, because they only award certification for lengthy courses of study that require substantial capital investments. A more modularized system would move beyond this all-or-nothing approach. Instead of taking general education classes for two years and then dropping out and ending up with little to show for their efforts except two years of debt, students could make smaller investments—in money and time—to acquire specific credentials.

This approach would also encourage students to think more strategically about specific learning paths to pursue, and make it easier to integrate internships into their education. Instead of randomly choosing courses to fulfill "general education" and "support courses" requirements, a student on a more modularized path might focus on, say, the six courses necessary to earn a certificate in "Workplace Communication Skills" or "The Future of Space Exploration." And then complete an associated internship before moving on to subsequent certificate programs.

At LinkedIn, we've developed a broad "Skills & Expertise" taxonomy that our members use to describe their attributes, and which then serve as the basis for endorsements from colleagues. For example, some of my skills include "Entrepreneurship," "Project Management," and "Viral Marketing." In a more outsourced form of Apple University, the in-house program that Apple now uses to teach its executives to think more like Steve Jobs, companies could use this taxonomy to publicize the skills and experiences they value most, and education providers could develop curricula that leads to certification in these areas.

For champions of a traditional liberal arts education, encouraging our nation's youth to major in "Project Management for Yahoo!" may sound like a higher education inferno even Dante himself couldn't stomach.

As certification gets more granular ... and as diplomas contain more information and exist as part of a larger, networked ecosystem, new possibilities emerge.

But the national mandate to produce more college graduates—as expressed by President Obama and many others—doesn't arise from our imminent shortage of Comp Lit majors. It arises from our desire to give more people access to training that can put them on a path to economic security, and to help them develop the skills that can keep America competitive on a global level.

Diplomas that get updated over time as new certificates are added, and which exist as part of larger certification platform, could transform the ways that employers use diplomas. Traditionally, bachelor's degrees have offered an easy way to winnow a pile of a thousand resumes into a pile of twenty resumes—but they're also a very limited filter. Because the specific information they codify about a person is minimal, they're far more useful for weeding than finding.

As certification gets more granular, however, and as diplomas contain more information and exist as part of a larger, networked ecosystem, new possibilities emerge. Want to find ten potential employees who have amassed at least three certificates related to brand management and have at least five positive endorsements from their instructors? A 21st century diploma should allow you to do that.

The Diploma as Platform

One of the main reasons the college degree persists as a technology is because it doesn't need a user manual. We know what a traditional college degree signifies in general. We're familiar with many of its nuances. A degree in Biochemistry & Molecular Biophysics from CalTech means one thing. A degree in Sculpture from Bennington means something else.

How, in a landscape of infinite certificates, will we determine which ones to value and trust? This is the problem that has always plagued alternate forms of certification, and it will only intensify as digital instruction becomes more full-featured and effective.

One organization trying to bring a sense of order to the imminent chaos is Mozilla, the non-profit that oversees the development of the open-source web browser, Firefox, and where I'm on the Board of Directors. In 2011, Mozilla introduced Open Badges, an initiative to develop free software and an open technical standard that any organization or individual can use to issue verified digital badges that symbolize a skill or achievement attained through either online or offline study or participation in some activity.

For example, you might earn a badge for completing a six-week "Introduction to Statistics" course, or for consistently making high-value contributions to an online message board where math students seek help on their homework.

As a person earns badges from multiple sources, they're all stored in a private repository called the Mozilla Backpack. There, you can arrange your badges into themed groups and choose which ones to share on social networks and other sites. Each badge comes with a great deal of metadata attached to it, including information about the issuer, what the badge signifies, the criteria used to assess your achievements, and on some occasions, links to the work you did in pursuit of the badge.

Already, Peer to Peer University, the YMCA of Greater New York, the Corporation for Public Broadcasting, and Disney-Pixar, to name just a few, have issued or are developing badges using Mozilla's technical standard. Mozilla is a good initial step, but there are many attributes that are important—ranging from employer trust to persistent storage of the certification if the source goes away—that still need to be worked out.

Creating a shared standard for attaching machine-readable information to certifications is an important first step for getting employer buy-in. Another key step will involve aggregating this data. If millions of people start storing their certification information in a common repository like LinkedIn, certification will evolve from a product (i.e., a traditional diploma) into a platform that can be easily searched and analyzed.

With certification as a platform, not just a product, the feedback loops between all parties will tighten. Education providers will have more capacity to track what employers are looking for and adjust their curricula accordingly. Students will have more explicit guideposts to follow, so they can invest their tuition dollars and time into developing skills that will truly increase their chances of transitioning successfully to the workforce. Employers will be able to use certification as a finding mechanism, not just a screening mechanism.

With certification as a platform, "Weed out everyone who doesn't have an Ivy League diploma" will evolve into "Let's find someone who possesses these specific skills and attributes that will help our organization." With certification as a platform, the communication device currently known as the 'diploma' becomes a much richer signal that will help businesses hire better and help individuals learn and grow faster.

Making this transition won't happen overnight. But if we truly want to use technology to transform higher education, we can't just confine our efforts to transforming instruction. We have to transform certification too. In doing so, we have an opportunity to create a new system that makes it clear to students what skills are most relevant and in highest demand, and thus gives them a chance to pursue these skills more strategically.

But our higher education system can't implement such changes alone. The business world has to embrace certification-as-a-platform, too. As long as it continues to depend on a 12th century communications device, the diploma, as its preferred gateway to entry, we won't be able to fully capitalize on 21st century innovations in technology and education.

Organizations to Contact

The editors have compiled the following list of organizations concerned with the issues debated in this book. The descriptions are derived from materials provided by the organizations. All have publications or information available for interested readers. The list was compiled on the date of publication of the present volume; the information provided here may change. Be aware that many organizations take several weeks or longer to respond to inquiries, so allow as much time as possible.

Brookings Institution
1775 Massachusetts Ave. NW, Washington, DC   20036
(202) 797-6000
e-mail: communications@brookings.edu
website: www.brookings.edu

The Brookings Institution is a nonprofit public policy organization that conducts independent research. The Brookings Institution uses its research to provide recommendations that advance the goals of strengthening American democracy, fostering social welfare and security, and securing a cooperative international system. The Brookings Institution publishes a variety of research papers, blogs, and opinion pieces available at its website, including "Why You Should Go to College."

Center for American Progress
1333 H St. NW, 10th Floor, Washington, DC   20005
(202) 682-1611
website: www.americanprogress.org

The Center for American Progress is a nonprofit, nonpartisan organization dedicated to improving the lives of Americans through progressive ideas and action. The organization dialogues with leaders, thinkers, and citizens to explore the vital issues facing America and the world. The Center for American Progress publishes numerous research papers, which are available at its website, including "College for All: Strengthening Our Economy Through College for All."

Center for College Affordability and Productivity (CCAP)
1055 Thomas Jefferson St. NW, Suite L 26
Washington, DC   20007
(202) 621-0536
e-mail: theccap@gmail.com
website: www.centerforcollegeaffordability.org

The Center for College Affordability and Productivity (CCAP) is dedicated to researching the rising costs and stagnant efficiency in higher education, with special emphasis on the United States. CCAP seeks to facilitate a broader dialogue on the issues and problems facing the institutions of higher education with the public, policy makers, and the higher education community. CCAP publishes a blog and a variety of policy papers, including "Why Are Recent College Graduates Underemployed?"

Georgetown University Center on Education and the Workforce
3300 Whitehaven St. NW, Suite 3200, Washington, DC   20007
(202) 687-7766 • fax: (202) 687-4999
e-mail: cewgeorgetown@georgetown.edu
website: https://cew.georgetown.edu

The Georgetown University Center on Education and the Workforce is an independent, nonprofit research and policy institute affiliated with the Georgetown McCourt School of Public Policy that studies the link between education, career qualifications, and workforce demands. The Center conducts research in three core areas with the goal of better aligning education and training with workforce and labor market demand: jobs, skills, and people. The Center publishes a variety of reports, including "The Economic Value of College Majors."

The Institute for College Access & Success (TICAS)
405 14th St., Suite 1100, Oakland, CA   94612
(510) 318-7900 • fax: (510) 318-7918
website: www.ticas.org

The Institute for College Access & Success (TICAS) works to make higher education more available and affordable for people of all backgrounds. TICAS conducts and supports nonpartisan research, analysis, and advocacy. TICAS has a variety of reports available at its website, such as "Student Debt and the Class of 2013."

Institute for Higher Education Policy (IHEP)
1825 K St. NW, Suite 720, Washington, DC   20006
(202) 861-8223 • fax: (202) 861-9307
e-mail: institute@ihep.org
website: www.ihep.org

The Institute for Higher Education Policy (IHEP) is a nonpartisan, nonprofit organization committed to promoting access to and success in higher education for all students. IHEP is committed to equality of opportunity for all and helps low-income, minority, and other historically underrepresented populations gain access to and achieve success in higher education. IHEP aims to enhance college affordability by reshaping college finance systems and publishes reports such as "The Investment Payoff: Reassessing and Supporting Efforts to Maximize the Benefits of Higher Education for Underserved Populations."

Lumina Foundation
30 S Meridian, Suites 700-800, Indianapolis, IN   46206-1806
(800) 834-5756
website: www.luminafoundation.org

Lumina Foundation is an independent, private foundation committed to increasing the proportion of Americans with high-quality degrees, certificates, and other credentials to 60 percent by 2025. Lumina Foundation focuses on helping to design and build an accessible, responsive, and accountable higher education system. Lumina Foundation's annual signature report, *A Stronger Nation Through Higher Education*, tracks progress toward Goal 2025.

National Education Association (NEA)

1201 16th St. NW, Washington, DC   20036-3290
(202) 833-4000 • fax: (202) 822-7974
website: www.nea.org

The National Education Association (NEA) is an educator membership organization that works to advance the rights of educators and children. The NEA focuses its energy on improving the quality of teaching, increasing student achievement, and making schools safe places to learn. The NEA also concentrates on issues of higher education, and within its Degrees Not Debt Campaign are a variety of media on the issue of student loans.

New America Foundation

1899 L St. NW, Suite 400, Washington, DC   20036
(202) 986-2700 • fax: (202) 986-3696
website: www.newamerica.org

The New America Foundation is a nonprofit, nonpartisan public policy institute that invests in new thinkers and new ideas to address the next generation of challenges facing the United States. The New America Foundation's Postsecondary National Policy Institute serves as a source of professional development for congressional staff working on higher education issues. Among its many publications available at its website is the primer "Federal Student Aid: A Background Primer."

Progressive Policy Institute (PPI)

1200 New Hampshire Ave. NW, Suite 575
Washington, DC   20036
(202) 525-3926 • fax: (202) 525-3941
website: www.ppionline.org

The Progressive Policy Institute (PPI) is a nonprofit organization that works to advance progressive, market-friendly ideas that promote American innovation, economic growth, and wider opportunity. PPI focuses on the four main areas of competitiveness, energy, medical innovation, and housing and financial services. Numerous articles can be found on the PPI website, including such titles as "College—Worth It or Worth Less?"

US Department of Education
400 Maryland Ave. SW, Washington, DC   20202
(800) 872-5327
website: www.ed.gov

The US Department of Education was established with the goal of improving education nationwide through the use of federally mandated education programs. The US Department of Education manages the Federal Student Aid office. Its website has a variety of information on student loans and manages the *FAFSA®* or *Free Application for Federal Student Aid.*

Bibliography

Books

Elizabeth A. Armstrong and Laura T. Hamilton	*Paying for the Party: How College Maintains Inequality.* Cambridge, MA: Harvard University Press, 2013.
Richard Arum and Josipa Roksa	*Aspiring Adults Adrift: Tentative Transitions of College Graduates.* Chicago: University of Chicago Press, 2014.
Antje Barabasch and Felix Rauner	*Work and Education in America: The Art of Integration.* New York: Springer Science and Business, 2012.
William J. Bennett and David Wilezol	*Is College Worth It? A Former United States Secretary of Education and a Liberal Arts Graduate Expose the Broken Promise of Higher Education.* Nashville, TN: Thomas Nelson, 2013.
Joel Best and Eric Best	*The Student Loan Mess: How Good Intentions Created a Trillion-Dollar Problem.* Berkeley: University of California Press, 2014.
Goldie Blumenstyk	*American Higher Education in Crisis? What Everyone Needs to Know.* New York: Oxford University Press, 2015.
Martin J. Bradley, Robert H. Seidman, and Steven R. Painchaud	*Saving Higher Education: The Integrated, Competency-Based Three-Year Bachelor's Degree Program.* San Francisco: Jossey-Bass, 2012.

Alan Collinge

The Student Loan Scam: The Most Oppressive Debt in US History, and How We Can Fight Back. Boston: Beacon Press, 2009.

Michael M. Crow and William B. Dabars

Designing the New American University. Baltimore, MD: Johns Hopkins University Press, 2015.

William Deresiewicz

Excellent Sheep: The Miseducation of the American Elite and the Way to a Meaningful Life. New York: Free Press, 2014.

Andrew Hacker and Claudia Dreifus

Higher Education? How Colleges Are Wasting Our Money and Failing Our Kids—And What We Can Do About It. New York: Times Books, 2010.

Brad J. Hershbein and Kevin M. Hollenbeck, eds.

Student Loans and the Dynamics of Debt. Kalamazoo, MI: Upjohn Institute, 2015.

Anya Kamenetz

How Our Future Was Sold Out for Student Loans, Credit Cards, Bad Jobs, No Benefits, and Tax Cuts for Rich Geezers—And How to Fight Back. New York: Riverhead Books, 2007.

Michael W. Kirst and Mitchell L. Stevens

Remaking College: The Changing Ecology of Higher Education. Stanford, CA: Stanford University Press, 2015.

Suzanne Mettler

Degrees of Inequality: How the Politics of Higher Education Sabotaged the American Dream. New York: Basic Books, 2014.

Glenn H. Reynolds	*The Higher Education Bubble.* New York: Encounter Books, 2012.
Bradley C.S. Watson	*The Idea of the American University.* Lanham, MD: Littlefield Publishers, 2011.
Robert Zemsky	*Checklist for Change: Making American Higher Education a Sustainable Enterprise.* New Brunswick, NJ: Rutgers University Press, 2013.

Periodicals and Internet Sources

Beth Akers and Matthew M. Chingos	"Is a Student Loan Crisis on the Horizon?," Brown Center on Education Policy at Brookings, June 2014. www.brookings.edu.
American Student Assistance	"Life Delayed: The Impact of Student Debt on the Daily Lives of Young Americans," 2013. www.asa.org.
Susan de Baca	"The 12 Hidden College Expenses," *Time,* November 16, 2012.
Victoria Bekiempis	"College Is *Still* a Waste of Time and Money," *Village Voice,* March 30, 2012.
Judah Bellin	"Is the Higher Education Bubble Finally Bursting?," *Washington Examiner,* November 14, 2013.

Anthony P. Carnevale, Stephen J. Rose, and Ban Cheah

"The College Payoff: Education, Occupations and Lifetime Earnings," Georgetown University Center on Education and the Workforce, 2011. https://cew.georgetown.edu.

Ann Coles

"The Investment Payoff: Reassessing and Supporting Efforts to Maximize the Benefits of Higher Education for Underserved Populations," Institute for Higher Education Policy, April 2013. www.ihep.org.

Peter Coy

"College Is a Waste—But Not Going Is Worse," *Bloomberg Business*, February 13, 2014. www.bloomberg.com.

Chris Denhart

"How the $1.2 Trillion College Debt Crisis Is Crippling Students, Parents and the Economy," *Forbes*, August 7, 2013.

Economist

"Is College Worth It?," April 5, 2014.

Max Ehrenfreund

"Private Colleges Are a Waste of Money for White, Middle Class Kids," *Washington Post*, December 18, 2014.

Josh Freedman

"Why American Colleges Are Becoming a Force for Inequality," *Atlantic*, May 16, 2013.

Michael Greenstone and Adam Looney

"Rising Student Debt Burdens: Factors Behind the Phenomenon," The Hamilton Project, July 5, 2013. www.brookings.edu.

Karen Herzog	"Working Your Way Through College Doesn't Add Up for Today's Students," *Milwaukee Wisconsin Journal Sentinel*, June 1, 2013.
Chris Isaac	"Voices: Don't Waste Your Time on Easy Classes," *USA Today*, October 23, 2014.
Gary Jason	"Approaching Crunch Time on the Student Loan Debacle," *American Thinker*, November 26, 2012. www.americanthinker.com.
Robert Kuttner	"Education Alone Is Not the Answer to Income Inequality and Slow Recovery," *American Prospect*, August 14, 2014.
Amy Laitinen	"College Credit? Kill That," CNN, March 30, 2015. www.cnn.com.
Megan McArdle	"Megan McArdle on the Coming Burst of the College Bubble," *Newsweek*, September 8, 2012.
Lawrence Mishel	"Education Is Not the Cure for High Unemployment or for Income Inequality," *EPI Briefing Paper*, no. 286, January 12, 2011. www.epi.org.
S. Georgia Nugent	"College Is Not a 'Ludicrous Waste of Money,'" *Huffington Post*, September 8, 2014. www.huffingtonpost.com.
Sophie Quinton	"Why You Might Be Paying Student Loans Until You Retire (and Beyond)," *National Journal*, September 18, 2014.

Cecilia Capuzzi Simon	"R.O.I.," *New York Times*, July 22, 2011.
Jackson Toby	"The Looming Student Loan Crisis," *The American*, May 14, 2013.
Brad Tuttle	"Congratulations, College Graduates! But Did You Just Waste Your Money, and Four Years of Your Lives?," *Time*, May 31, 2011.
Richard Vedder and Christopher Denhart	"How the College Bubble Will Pop," *Wall Street Journal*, January 8, 2014.
Jordan Weissmann	"Our Student Loan System Is Broken, and These New Statistics Prove It," *Atlantic*, August 8, 2013.
Gillian B. White	"Even with Debt, College Still Pays Off," *Atlantic*, February 20, 2015.
Luigi Zingales	"The College Graduate as Collateral," *New York Times*, June 14, 2012.

Index

CPSIA information can be obtained
at www.ICGtesting.com
Printed in the USA
FFOW01n2158180416
23309FF